GARY PLAYER'S GOLF SECRETS

GARY PLAYER'S

PRENTICE-HALL, INC., ENGLEWOOD CLIFFS, N. J.

GOLF SECRETS

Gary Player.

Gary Player's Golf Secrets *by Gary Player*

Second printing........April, 1966

FOREWORD

AFTER "baring my soul" in the preparation of this book, I find it very difficult to present observations about myself or my golf game that are not already covered in the pages that follow.

However, I would like to take this opportunity to tell what I tried to accomplish in this book—and what I tried to avoid.

I think a beginning player could read this book and be helped considerably. There is basic instruction that is presented to teach the beginner or high handicap player and to remind the more proficient golfer.

However, this book is primarily devoted to the golfer who wishes to play championship golf—the reader who will be willing to work on his game; the player who is interested in the little extra things that will move him from Class A to Championship Flight in his club tournaments.

Therefore, I dwell considerably on the incidentals—the gimmicks—which help touring professionals lower their scores that all-important two or three shots per round.

There are many "truths" in golf which dictate the correct method of striking a ball. However, I feel there are also many areas of golf on which I should not dictate to a reader, because I cannot be on hand personally to note that person's physical qualifications and swing habits.

When discussing such areas of the swing I have tried to make it clear that my suggestions are based on what works in my swing. When possible I have pointed out what might work better for someone of different physique and skill.

Therefore I would advise that the readers of this, or any, golf book should pick and choose what is most help-ful and applicable to their respective games. Then the reader should discuss with his professional what he has read in order to correctly incorporate the author's think-ing into his swing.

I learned my golf largely by picking and choosing from what I had read and heard from others, discarding what I thought was not correct or applicable to my game, and re-taining that which I felt would help me.

As a result I feel that though my swing may not be con-sidered orthodox (I don't really believe there is an ortho-dox golf swing), it is a swing that remains constant and workable. I started this book in the spring of 1961, just after winning the Masters, and it is amazing to me that, upon re-reading the early chapters, there is practically nothing about which I have changed my thinking.

It would be impossible for me to list all of the people who have helped me in my career as a golfer; however, I would like to give special mention to a few.

First I wish to thank my father, a two-handicap player who started me in golf and who had enough confidence in my game to take an overdraft on his bank account to help sponsor me on my first world tour.

I have received helpful advice and encouragement from many people in golf but one who stands out most in my mind is my father-in-law Jock Vervey. I am very grateful to him and also to the members at the Killarney Country Club of Johannesburg who helped support me on my first trip abroad.

When speaking of encouragement I cannot overlook all the friends in the United States, England and all over the world who have made this foreigner feel at home in their company.

I think my wife, Vivienne, already knows how much I appreciate the wonderful role she has played as a wife and mother, but I would like to make it public. Traveling with three children and a nurse, life would really be hectic for me if it were not for Viv's patience and understanding. She never complains.

Finally I want to thank my good friend Dick Aultman and the staff at *Golf Digest* magazine for their expert help in the preparation of this book.

GARY PLAYER
June, 1962

CONTENTS

GARY PLAYER'S GOLF SECRETS

CHAPTER **1**

DRIVING FOR DISTANCE

AFTER THE 1960 Masters tournament I told myself, "Gary, if you ever expect to win this championship you'd better add at least 30 yards to your drives."

I had just finished my fourth try at the Masters, and the reason for my failure to win was obvious to me. I just couldn't reach most of the par-5 holes in two shots. Instead of putting for eagles on these holes as Arnold Palmer was doing, I was being forced to rely on a full approach and a good putt to get even a birdie.

By the time of the 1961 Masters, I was hitting at least 30 yards farther than in 1960. As a result I was capable of reaching the par-5s at Augusta in two shots, unless I was hitting into the wind. This added length helped me immeasurably in winning the tournament.

Certainly extra distance is a primary factor at Augusta, but it plays an even more important role at other courses on the United States pro tour.

Many of these events are played on wide-open municipal courses where the premium is on distance, rather than accuracy.

The lack of sand and rough on these courses is by design and is understandable. Courses in the United States are overcrowded now, and operators do not want play slowed even more by persons searching for balls.

I do think, however, that this type of course gives the golf "slugger" an advantage he would not have on the narrow fairways of private clubs, where tournaments are held elsewhere in the world.

I can safely say that if all American tournaments were played on truly championship courses, such as those on which the U.S. Open, Masters, and PGA championship are played, you would find some leading money-winners finishing as "also-rans." This becomes obvious when you note how rarely anyone but a truly skilled shotmaker wins one of these three major events.

Keeping in mind this American stress on the long ball, I hope my methods of adding distance will be helpful to the reader.

First, I had all of my clubs made one-half inch longer than the standard length I had been using. Longer clubs naturally give a longer swing arc. If you have a longer arc in golf you're automatically going to hit the ball farther.

Also, with longer clubs it is possible to shorten your grip on the shaft if a shot calls for less distance; with a short club you don't have enough shaft to grip farther up when you need extra length.

A word of warning: the prospective club buyer who wants more length should consult his professional for advice before investing in longer shafts.

A second factor that helped me hit the ball farther was improvement of my weight shift. Like many golfers, I had a problem shifting my weight to my left foot on the down-

Two drawings show incorrect (left) and correct positions at finish of swing. Incorrect drawing shows too much weight still on right side. The golfer has probably released his wrists too early on downswing, causing loss of clubhead speed and probably a sliced shot. Correct drawing shows weight on left foot with hip and shoulder turn completed. Such a finished position indicates that weight shifted to left early on downswing and that proper "delayed" release of wrists occurred.

swing. I frequently fell back on my right leg, pulling away from the ball. Your weight should move slightly to the right foot on the backswing and then shift to the left foot immediately at the start of the downswing.

The one thing I concentrate on during my swing is shifting my weight to the left foot in returning the clubhead to the ball.

This weight shift to the left adds distance because it helps delay the uncocking of the wrists on the downswing. This "delayed hit" uncocks the wrists just before impact so that the speed of the clubhead really accelerates as it meets the ball.

Too many golfers feel they add distance by swinging harder with hands and arms. They start the downswing with their hands and arms before shifting their weight to the left foot. As a result they uncock their wrists too early, wasting clubhead speed.

Uncocking the wrists with a delayed hit is the real secret of long drives, but you shouldn't be conscious of hands and arms in the golf swing. By immediately shifting your weight forward on the downswing, you will automatically delay unlocking your wrists. Your hands and arms will follow your hip turn naturally and whip the club through.

A proper weight shift brings the big muscles into play and provides a delayed uncocking of the wrists on the downswing. You will find it can do wonders in adding distance.

Paul Harney is an excellent example of a golfer who uses the proper weight shift. Paul is slight, weighing about 140 pounds. Yet, he is one of the longest hitters in golf. That length helps him to average more than $20,000 in earnings a year on the professional tour.

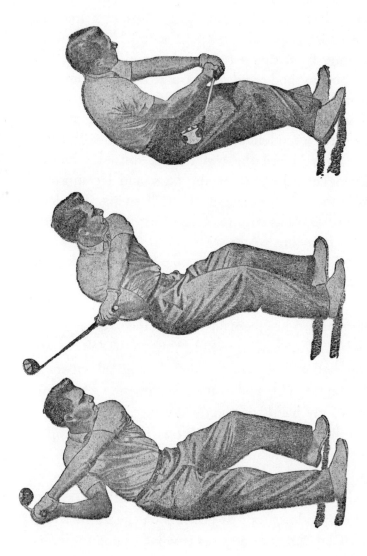

Drawings show crucial area in Gary Player's swing. At top of backswing (first drawing) his weight is largely on his right foot. As downswing begins (second drawing), his left heel lowers; hips begin turn to left; right knee moves toward target, and right elbow returns to right side. Wrists are still cocked. As hands and clubhead enter hitting area (third drawing), right arm begins to straighten and wrists start to uncock. Weight has shifted to left side, which leads clubhead into the ball.

17

Here is how I achieve my weight shift on drives:

I close my stance, which means my right foot is pulled back farther than my left from along the target line. In this stance, it is easier for me to get a full body turn on the backswing. By taking a full windup and by using the big muscles of my body and legs, I add both rhythm and power to my swing.

Golfers who start the club back with their hands and arms alone have a tendency to swing at the ball with their hands and arms before the weight has shifted forward. Thus, they never fully employ the back and leg muscles that provide maximum power in the golf swing. The legs are about four times as strong as the arms: why waste this potential by swinging solely with hands and arms?

The closed stance also helps me take the club back well inside the line to the target. This prevents me from returning the clubhead to the ball from the outside, thus creating a sliced shot and consequent loss of distance.

I also help my downswing weight shift to the left by addressing the ball with my left toe slightly pointed outward, toward the target. This makes it easier for me to turn my hips ahead of my hands on the downswing.

Several other features of my address foster this proper weight shift and the resulting delayed hit.

I like to imagine my right elbow is against my side at address, although physically it isn't. I want this elbow tucked into my side as soon as possible on the downswing, so that what I'm doing at address is what I hope to duplicate at impact.

This is also true of my right leg, which I bow slightly forward at address, pointing the knee a bit toward target.

As with the right elbow, this merely advances the position I want to be in when I hit the ball.

These actions, the right elbow in tight, and kicking the right knee toward the target, help me transfer my weight to my left foot.

The legs play a big part in the golf swing. Lively legs are needed to get a full windup on the backswing and proper weight shift coming down. Golf is like most other sports—tennis, boxing, swimming, baseball, and even dancing—in that strong, active legs are important for rhythm and weight transfer.

Jumping rope and doing some skipping every day is one of the best ways of making the legs strong and supple.

Being relaxed at the address position also makes it easier to shift the weight during the swing. I like to take a deep breath and exhale before I start the action, as many baseball pitchers do before they throw. I then make my forward press, kick my right knee and hands a bit more toward target, and follow with the backswing.

Maintenance of good physical condition has helped me hit the ball farther. I watch my diet very closely and follow an exercise routine. Playing golf almost every day, year after year, keeping in shape both mentally and physically becomes not only important, it is essential.

I really enjoy exercise. Sometimes after a bad day on the course I come home tired and discouraged. But if I exercise before going to bed, I feel clean and strong again. This does wonders for me mentally, as well as physically.

I do 60 or 70 fingertip pushups daily. However, I refrain from these rigorous exercises just before a round of golf because they tend to make my muscles stiff. I also do knee bends to keep my legs in shape.

A book on yoga has been a big help. It taught me the benefits of standing on my head at least two minutes each day. This pumps blood to my brain (the most important organ in the body—even for a golfer[!]) and makes me more alert for the day ahead. I never sleep with a pillow. I believe a pillow only makes it more difficult for my heart to pump blood to my brain.

I refrain from sweets, pastries, and fried foods. On the course I like to eat dried fruits. Like Napoleon, I believe that an "army marches on its stomach," and that the fruits I eat during a round of golf help me build energy. They give the acids in my stomach something to work on.

Believe me, I think the way some people fail to take care of their bodies is terrible. When I put on swim trunks, I want to look nice and trim. I like to see women with nice figures, and I imagine they like to see men who are well built. When I'm 50 I don't expect to weigh much more than I do now (about 160).

Now that I've discussed things that have helped me hit the ball farther, I think I'd better point out a few dangers a golfer seeking greater distance must try to avoid.

First, you may find you are going too high on your left toe when you try a full windup on the backswing. You will see from pictures of my swing that I am somewhat guilty of this myself.

However, if you must lift your left heel high on the backswing, be certain you lower it immediately at the start of the downswing. If you don't, your weight may remain on your right foot and you will automatically fall back, uncocking your wrists too early. You will find yourself throwing the club out with your hands as if you were casting a

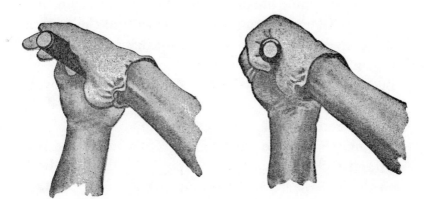

Possible pitfall in striving for extra distance. In drawing at left, the golfer has allowed club to slip in left hand at top of backswing. Correct drawing at right shows club held firmly in last three fingers of his hand.

flyrod, instead of bringing them in close to your body in the delayed hit position.

Some people trying for extra distance have a tendency to overswing. They take the club back farther than they should. Guard against opening your left hand at the top of your backswing. You cannot overswing if this hand grips the club firmly throughout the swing. (Reverse for a left-hander, of course).

A second pitfall in striving for length is a tendency to swing the shoulders on too level a plane. The left shoulder should tilt slightly on the backswing, and the right shoulder should swing well down and under on the downswing.

In closing, I'd like to talk about hitting the ball hard. Watching me play, you might say I swing hard. This is true. Actually, I feel that I am swinging as hard as I can.

It's a funny thing about golfers. Many won't admit they swing as hard as they can, within reason. But the truth is that all the players on the pro tour hit that ball as hard as they can and still keep it in play.

But swinging hard at the ball doesn't in itself provide distance. It is the proper weight shift and the delayed hit that gives results—as I mentioned earlier.

You must also have good timing. To swing at the ball hard and still maintain good timing, take the club back from the ball slowly. Build your swing up slowly, with a full body turn, a firm grip, and then zoom into the ball.

From the day I started golf, I've always tried to hit the ball as hard as I could; I would advise that any young boy or girl who is beginning golf do the same. It's simple to go from a hard swing to an easier one. But, if you have been an easy swinger, it's difficult to suddenly start hitting the ball hard. More often it goes the other way, and an easy swinger develops a lazy stroke when he gets older.

DRIVING FOR DISTANCE CHECKPOINTS

✔ Longer length clubs can produce a wider swing arc and add distance, but consult your pro before buying.

✔ Your weight should shift to your right foot on the backswing and immediately to your left foot at the start of the downswing.

✔ Proper weight shift produces delayed uncocking of wrists on downswing.

✔ Proper weight shift encourages full body windup and use of large muscles in legs and back.

✔ Closed stance helps produce inside takeaway and full body coiling on backswing.

✔ Pointing left toe slightly toward target encourages uncoiling and weight shift to left leg on downswing.

✔ When striving for distance, guard against:
   —Lifting left heel too high on backswing and failing to lower it at start of downswing.
   —A loose grip on club with left hand at top of backswing.
   —Turning shoulders on a level plane instead of tilting them slightly on backswing and bringing right shoulder down and under on downswing.

CHAPTER 2

FAIRWAY SHOTS— DON'T BE GREEDY

THE BEST advice I can give any golfer about playing fairway shots is: *Don't Be Greedy*.

I honestly feel that if I could caddie for an average golfer, I could cut several strokes from his normal score— without giving him a single tip about his swing. I would save him strokes by handing him the right club for each fairway shot situation.

I've seen it happen time and again in pro-amateur tournaments: an amateur with whom I'm playing finds his ball in a bad lie, well down in the grass, about 220 yards from the green. He knows the close lie demands using a 4-wood or 2-iron, but he also realizes he can't reach the green with anything except a perfect 2-wood shot.

So he swings the less lofted brassie, tops the shot and finds himself still needing a long iron to reach the green. Still cursing his bad luck with the brassie, he bangs away —often into a sand trap near the green. The result is often a six or seven on the hole.

Had he played a 2-iron or a 4- or 5-wood from the bad

lie, he might have scored a four or at worst a five, depending on whether he needed one or two putts after chipping to the green.

Similar situations, when it is wiser to play a safe shot, occur in every round of golf.

The next time you compete, try playing the safest shot every time. There may be an occasion when the gamble might pay off, but on the whole you will score lower because you will have eliminated the double and triple bogies.

I, for one, don't even carry a 2-wood in my bag. It's much easier and safer to use a 3- or 4-wood.

Judging distance is an important phase of your fairway game and one that poses a problem for high and low handicap players alike.

Recall your last round of golf: count the number of times your approach shots finished short of the green. And how many times did they go over? If you are typical of most amateurs, you were short more times than not.

Think about the course you played. Was the trouble on most of the holes in front of or behind the greens? On the majority of courses the trouble is in front. So why be short?

Almost all golfers with handicaps of five or higher could move down to one less lofted iron (or wood if the ball's lie is good) than they would normally use for a shot to the green.

There are several gimmicks the touring pros use to help judge distance. One of these is called "progression."

Progression is helpful on shots to a green where the distance is deceiving because of undulations in the fairway. In judging distance by progression, I select an object which is about wedge distance from my ball to the hole. This

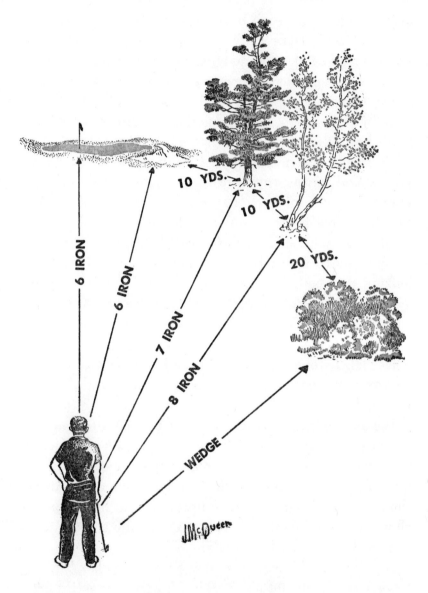

"Progression" method of judging distance: Gary sights object that is wedge-distance away. Then he picks out other objects that are progressively closer to the target. By dropping down one less lofted club for each 10-yard segment his sightings progress from ball, he finally arrives at correct club with which to reach the green.

object could be a tree, a bush, or a blemish in the fairway.

I know that I have a full wedge because, like most golfers, I have little trouble judging distance on such a short shot. I also know that for every 10 yards I increase my distance, I must step down to one less lofted club.

So by progression, I select another object about 10 or 20 yards beyond the first and estimate it would require a 9 or an 8-iron to reach that spot. I continue to pick objects farther and farther from my ball, progressing one lower-numbered club for each 10 yards of distance added. By the time I reach the green, I have a pretty good idea of what club I will need for the actual shot.

Sometimes I find it helpful to judge distance merely by looking at something near the green, such as a tree or the gallery. By focusing on such an object, other than the flag, I can clear doubts about the distance to the hole.

If there is a sand trap in front of the green, I imagine what club I would need to land the ball in the trap. Then I move down one less lofted club to make certain I clear the bunker.

We all encounter situations where it seems a toss-up between using, say, a 4 or a 5-iron. When I am in doubt, I usually choose the one with more loft because it will require a firmer stroke to reach the target. One of the worst things a golfer can do is ease up on a shot. So if you do choose the less lofted club, make certain you shorten your grip and stroke the ball firmly.

A golfer should never quit using a certain club because he believes he cannot use it well. It's best to practice with that club until you master it. If you ignore the inability to hit with a certain club, chances are your swing errors are causing trouble that will creep into the rest of your game.

The question that arises in discussions of fairway shots is whether or not a player should use the same swing with irons and fairway woods he employs on drives.

I feel the swing will differ between tee and fairway shots, primarily in its length. However, any swing differences are merely a direct result of playing with shorter clubs from turf, rather than with the longer drives from a tee.

I do not feel a player should consciously alter his swing for fairway shots. The only change involved should concern his position at address.

Normally, I play my fairway woods and long irons (1, 2 and 3) from the same stance as I do my drives, that is, directly opposite my left heel. I play these shots well forward, so I feel certain of getting them into the air. Putting long iron shots into flight is a big problem for some golfers, and I suggest to those who are bothered to try using a 5-wood, with its extra loft, instead of a 1, 2, or 3-iron.

I play the middle irons (4, 5, and 6) between my left heel and the center of my stance. I position the shorter, more lofted irons about the middle of my stance. My stance becomes slightly narrower and I stand closer to the ball with the more lofted irons.

My stance for various fairway shots is slightly different but my hands always remain the same. They are farther ahead of the ball on a short-iron shot which I play from a center stance than, say, on a 4-iron shot, with the ball farther forward. It is important to keep your hands ahead of the clubhead on the short irons so that you will hit down on the ball, rather than scoop behind it.

On all fairway shots, as when driving, I concentrate primarily on shifting my weight to my left foot early in the downswing. This minimizes the chance of falling back on the right foot and hitting behind the ball or topping it.

I take a divot on all fairway shots, even with woods. If I've shifted my weight left on the downswing, the clubhead will contact the ball and turf simultaneously. As I progress to the middle and shorter irons, the clubhead meets the ball before it does the turf. Thus, the divot mark will appear progressively farther ahead of ball position as I move down to the more lofted irons. This occurs naturally because I am playing these shots farther back toward the center of my stance and my hands are thus farther ahead of the ball.

There are occasions on fairway shots when a player should alter his club selection and address position. One of these situations occurs when the ball is in a bad lie, as in a divot mark. When this occurs, I use a more lofted club, because I know that with such a lie I will get less-than-normal height and also more roll because of less backspin. By using more loft I increase the height of the shot and lessen the distance.

Because I am using a more lofted club, I will play the ball a bit farther back in my stance and hit down on the shot more decidedly. In hitting from bad lies make certain to hit down and through the ball. If you try to scoop or sweep it out, you will probably top the ball.

Quite often on fairway shots a player must hit from the side of a hill. Remember that on hilly lies, the ball's flight will curve in the same direction the hill slopes. You must adjust your address to compensate for the ball's curve.

On a sidehill lie where the ball is above your feet— where the hill slopes to the left—your ball will also travel to the left of target, unless you aim further right to allow for the difference. On such shots you should also grip

Ball will curve in same direction that hill slopes, so aim to right of target and shorten grip when ball lies above feet (left). Aim left, grip at end of club when feet are above ball (right).

farther down the shaft to provide a flatter, baseball-like swing plane.

When your feet are above the ball in a sidehill lie, you can expect the ball to fly to the right because the hill slopes to that direction. So now aim to the left of target. And grip at the end of the shaft and stand a bit closer to the ball to accommodate a more upright swing.

I advocate no further alterations on sidehill shots, such as opening or closing your stance or changing your swing. Golf is complex enough without such unnecessary complications. Merely allow for the ball's curve, shorten or lengthen your grip to accommodate for a flatter or more upright swing.

On uphill or downhill lies, the slope again determines the ball's flight direction.

When you are hitting uphill, with your front foot higher than your back foot, you can expect a higher shot with less distance than normal. Thus you must step down to one less lofted club—or more if the slope is extreme—to get less height and more distance.

When hitting uphill, your clubhead will reach the ground a bit later in your swing, so you must position the ball a bit farther forward in your stance.

It is extremely important to shift your weight to the left on the downswing of an uphill shot. Otherwise you most certainly will fall and probably top the ball.

On downhill shots, when your rear foot is higher than your front, the opposite applies. Use a more lofted club to compensate for the lower flight of the ball; play the ball

Ball will fly higher and shorter than normal from uphill lie (left) so use less lofted club and play ball farther forward than usual. Use more loft, play ball back on downhill shot (right).

Player aims at flag which is guarded by hazard on the right, but he avoids open stance and outside takeaway which might produce a slice (right). Instead, he closes stance and takes club away from ball well inside target line (left).

farther back in your stance because your clubhead will reach the ground earlier on the downswing.

Another instance where my technique for fairway shots differs is when I'm faced with a shot to a pin that is to one side of a green, tucked behind a hazard.

Say the pin is on the right side of the green and guarded by a pond or sand trap. Here, I must not slice.

Popular strategy in such cases would call for a straight shot to the center or left-center of the green, avoiding the hazard. I feel this is risky, because a sliced shot would carry into the sand or water.

Instead, I aim directly at the pin, but I also alter my stance and backswing a bit to eliminate any chance of slicing. To do this I simply close my stance a bit, pulling the right foot back from the target line. I also take the clubhead back well inside the target line as I start the back-swing. This will insure against an outside-in path for the clubhead when it returns to the ball, and any slice spin this might produce.

If the flag were on the left side of the green and guarded by a hazard, I will want to protect against a hook. Again I aim for the flag. However, this time I open my stance, pulling my left foot (instead of the right) back from the target line. Also, I take the club straight back from the ball, or possibly slightly outside the target line, so my swing will not develop the inside-out pattern which might put a hook spin on the ball.

FAIRWAY SHOT CHECKPOINTS

- The 2-wood can be a dangerous club unless you have an excellent lie in the fairway. It's better to sacrifice a few yards' distance and avoid a miss-hit shot.

- Analyze your past rounds to see if you are in the habit of falling short on approach shots. If so, use more club in the future.

- When in doubt about the correct club, it's better to swing the more lofted club with a firm stroke than to ease up with less lofted club.

- Inability to hit a certain club correctly should be over-come, lest similar errors start showing with other clubs.

- A player should not consciously alter his swing when going from drives to fairway shots. However, some dif-ferences will naturally occur as one progresses to shots with shorter clubs and at a non-teed ball.

↙ The ball should be played farther back in the stance as one progresses to more lofted clubs. However, hands should remain in the same address position for all shots.

↙ Your divot mark should appear progressively farther ahead of the original ball position as you progress to more lofted clubs.

↙ Use a more lofted club from a bad lie because the ball will roll farther than normal.

↙ Grip shorter on club for sidehill lies when ball is above your feet. Grip at end of shaft when ball is below your feet.

↙ Use a less lofted club than normal and play ball forward in stance when hitting from an uphill lie. Use more loft and play ball back on downhill lies.

↙ On sidehill lies, the ball will tend to curve in the same direction that the hill slopes. It will fly higher and carry shorter than normal from uphill lies. It will fly lower and roll farther from downhill lies.

CHAPTER 3

CHIPPING AND PITCHING
FOR ONE PUTT

MY SON, Mark, can hardly hold a rattle, much less a golf club, so it will be some time before he takes up the game.

But when he does start, if I have anything to say about it—and I think I will—I'll make sure he begins with his short shots, the putts, chips and pitches.

I don't want him to fall into the bad habit of most week-end players, who feel that practicing isn't worthwhile un-less they stress drives and full iron shots.

Sure, driving is fun. I get just as big a thrill out of a well-hit tee shot as the next fellow. But the person who works on driving learns only how to drive—nothing else.

On the other hand, a person who works on his short shots, those around the green, learns not only this im-portant phase of the game, but also develops feel and rhythm. And these play a big part in *all* golf shots—yes, even the drive.

Every golfer on the tour—I don't care how well he hits the ball—is going to have days when he misses a lot of greens, and that is when he must rely on his short shots.

Chip and pitch shots are even more important for the weekend golfer, who misses more greens than does the touring pro. I can think of no quicker way to lower one's handicap than the ability to consistently chip close enough for one putt instead of two.

So let's do it!

First, we must understand the differences between the chip shot and the pitch.

A chip shot assumes a lower trajectory than the pitch because it is hit with a less lofted club. It can be expected to land on or just short of a green and roll to the hole with little backspin retarding its forward progress.

A pitch shot, hit with a more lofted club, flies high to the green, lands near the flagstick and, because of backspin, quickly comes to rest.

A variation of the normal pitch is the pitch-and-run shot which, though also highly lofted, lands short of a green and runs a bit to the flag. This shot is useful when hitting with a strong wind that minimizes backspin, or to a hard-baked green that will not hold a normal pitch.

Whenever feasible, any short shot—pitch or chip—should be played to land on the green. It's the best-groomed area on any golf course. So why take a chance on getting a bad bounce by playing short?

Far and away the most satisfactory method of stroking the ball to the hole from within 20 yards of the green is the chip shot.

On this shot I may use any club from a 4-iron through an 8-iron. The exact club selection depends on the specific shot situation—the lie of the ball in the grass, the length of the shot, the amount of green between the ball and the hole, the character of the green's turf, the terrain between the ball and the hole, and even the direction and velocity of the wind.

Generally speaking, a 4-iron will hit the green and roll farther than a 5-iron hit with the same force. The 5-iron runs farther than the 6-iron, and so on.

There is less chance of scuffing behind the ball with a less lofted club such as a 4-iron, than with, say, the more lofted 7-iron. Therefore, I always try to use the least lofted club which will take my ball onto the green in flight and still not let it roll past the hole.

As I choose my club for the shot, I also select an exact landing spot on the green. This spot may be a light or dark patch of grass, a cigarette ash, a clover leaf, anything to provide a target.

Selection of a landing spot is determined largely by the roll and texture of the green. I read the green, just as I would on a putt, and allow for any slopes. If the green slopes to the right, I naturally try to land my ball a bit to the left to play for the roll.

After sighting the landing spot, I take a few practice strokes alongside the ball. Each time I visualize the spot in my mind's eye and try to swing the club with just enough force to land the ball on that spot. Then I repeat the procedure with the actual shot, still seeing the spot in my mind.

For consistently fine chipping it is very important to always contact the ball first and then the turf.

To assure this, I make certain my hands are well forward of the clubhead, both at address and at impact. If I let my hands lag behind the clubhead, the lowest part of my swing will occur behind the ball.

To hit the ball first, I find it also helps to keep most of

my weight on my left foot (right foot for left-handers).

The word chip sounds the way the shot should be executed—a short, crisp, but rhythmical, stroke—much like slapping a baby on its bottom. The feet should be positioned about parallel with the line to the target. Since it is a short shot, the stance should be narrow with the hands near to the body. The knees should be bent to avoid tension in the legs. It's largely a hand and arm movement, with little or no body turn.

Because the hands and weight are forward, the club will come into the ball with a slightly downward movement.

When chipping, make certain you see the blade of the club hit the ball. Don't let your chin move forward before the hit. Hit past your chin and then follow the ball's flight.

Once you have mastered the chip stroke, your concentration should be entirely on hitting the spot where you want the ball to land.

Selecting the correct landing spot and the right club is half the battle in chipping. This requires a knowledge of what shot trajectory each club will produce and how far the ball will run. The only way to develop this sense is through practice.

I have actually measured the amount of roll I can expect on chips with different clubs and it might help for you to do the same.

For instance, when chipping to a level green of average texture from a normal lie, I know that my 6-iron shot will roll about twice as far as it flies—or two-thirds of the total distance to the hole. Thus, if I am 21 paces from the hole, I know I should land the ball on a spot seven paces from where it now lies. People may think I'm a bit off when they see me pacing the distance of the ball to the hole, counting to myself, but it does help me.

As I mentioned before, the chip shot is best when you have a great deal of green between you and the hole. It's a bad policy to use a pitch shot with a wedge or 9-iron in such a situation, because often the ball will take a great deal of backspin and stop short.

However, the short pitch is a valuable shot around the green when you must stop the ball in a hurry; such as when the green slopes away from your ball, or when you need a high shot to clear a sand trap with little green beyond.

When the green slopes upward from your ball and then levels off several feet before the hole, it may be safer to pitch over the slope to the level area than to chip into the slope and take a chance on the ball stopping short.

In pitching it is extremely important to note the texture of the green, especially near the flagstick where the ball should land. If the turf is unusually hard or soft in that area, you must play the shot to carry shorter or farther than normal.

This pitch is similar to the chip in that the stance should be narrow with the knees bent. Again, the weight should be largely on the forward foot with the hands ahead of the clubhead at all times until after impact. As with the chip, there should be little body movement and the ball should be struck first, with a downward stroke.

However, because I want this shot to fly high and stop quickly, I open my stance slightly so that my left foot is pulled back from the target line. This allows me to take the club back more to the outside than on the chip. The outside-in swing assures against hitting the ball with a closed clubface, which would reduce backspin.

Also on the pitch shot, I cock my wrists abruptly on the backswing. This makes my swing more upright and produces greater height and backspin. *It is the only shot in golf, aside from the blast from sand and the shot from heavy rough, wherein I use the early wrist cock.*

If extreme height is required on the shot, I will play the ball off my left foot, open my stance even more, and take the club back more outside with a sharper wrist cock. Thus, I hit this shot closer to the start of the upswing than the chip or average pitch, which are definitely hit on the downswing. As a result I contact the ball with an open blade and achieve even greater height.

There should be nothing lazy about your pitch swing. It should be rhythmical but with firm wrists. A lazy stroke may cause you to hit behind the ball.

The pitching wedge is a valuable club for the skilled player, and no group has mastered it better than the American professionals. Its extra weight and loft give added height and backspin to a properly-executed shot. However, the wedge can also be a dangerous club for the average weekend player unless he has practiced using it. In soggy turf he might leave it "sticking in the ground." On hard ground it can bounce or skid into the ball. So, unless you are skilled with this club, or unless you find your ball in an extremely good lie, you will be safer with a 9-iron.

The Texas wedge, as Americans have labeled the putter when it's used from off the green, can be a handy club if used in a correct situation. Many weekend players have more confidence in putting from off the green than in chipping. It is also a good club to use off bare ground from which a lofted club might bounce behind the ball.

Generally speaking, I will putt from off the green only

when my ball is within two feet of the edge, when the
fringe is fairly short and smooth, and when the ball is setting high on the grass.

I will not putt from the fringe when the ball is low in the
grass or when the grass lays in the opposite direction of
the shot.

For the shot, I use the same putting grip and stroke but
hit the ball slightly harder than normal to get it through
the fringe. I make certain I stroke through the putt and do
not stub my putter in the grass.

Some of the best players of short shots around the green
I have seen are Bobby Locke, Jerry Barber, Doug Ford
and Dow Finsterwald. All four stress the short game in
their practice.

In many respects learning to play golf is much like learn-

Gary advocates putting from the fringer when ball sits up in straight grass (left) or
rests in grass which lays in the same direction as the intended shot (to reader's right).

It is wise to leave putter in your bag when ball lies in fringe grass that lays in the
opposite direction of shot (left) or when ball rests low in fairly long grass (right).

ing to drive an automobile. A new driver gets a big kick out of taking dad's car onto a straight, open piece of highway. But all he learns is how to drive on straight, open highway.

By practicing turning and parking, he could develop skills of auto driving—a feel for the car—that also help on the open road.

So the next time you practice your golf, don't be like the new driver who starts on the straightaway. Forget about hitting so many tee shots.

Instead, work on the turning and parking phases of golf —the chip and pitch shots around the green. You will develop skills and feel and timing, which will also benefit your full iron and wood shots.

PITCHING AND CHIPPING CHECKPOINTS

✔ Practicing chip and pitch shots develops feel and rhythm that will also be helpful on full iron and wood shots.

✔ Select the least lofted club that will land your ball on the green without its rolling past the hole.

✔ Pick a spot on the green from which your ball will bounce and roll to the hole. Then land the ball on this spot.

✔ On chip and pitch shots, except where extreme height is required, always contact first the ball and then the turf.

✔ Keep your hands well ahead of the clubhead, both at address and impact.

🗸 Keep most of your weight on your left foot throughout the swing.

🗸 Swing mostly with your hands and arms. Employ only enough body and leg movement to provide rhythm.

🗸 The chip shot should be hit with a short, crisp stroke. The pitch shot requires a longer, rhythmical, but firm stroke with no collapsing of the arms or wrists.

CHAPTER 4

ON THE GREEN

I HAVE a very keen friend in Johannesburg named Fardel Allem. He and his family have a farm which, I would guess, is at least 20,000 acres.

When I go home to rest, I go to his farm, where Fardel has a big putting green, a sand trap, and a driving range in front of the house.

The real fun comes when Fardel and I putt against each other. When one of us loses, he must shake the winner's hand and say: "Sir, you are the greatest putter in the world." Both of us are very proud people so we practice very hard to make the other bow.

I'd like Fardel to know that the practice I have had on his putting green in our friendly but very serious matches indirectly helped me a great deal to win the Masters tournament.

I mention my putting matches with Fardel to illustrate the very important point that putting practice can be enjoyable as well as worthwhile.

If you don't think putting practice is important, compare the time the average touring professional spends on the practice green with time on the practice tee. I'm sure most pros, especially the more successful ones, spend as much, if not more, time on their putting than on all other shots combined.

This is logical when you consider that the scratch golfer takes almost as many shots on the green as he does from tee to green. The winner of a professional tournament will invariably acknowledge his putting was superior. It had to be: there are just as many other players who hit the ball equally well enroute to the green.

I must admit that there have been many times when I felt putting plays too important a role in golf. It doesn't seem right to me that a putt, hanging on the side of the cup because a spike mark kicked it off-line, should be as costly as a completely whiffed tee shot.

But I'm not going to start a campaign to devalue the putt. Golf would suffer immeasurably if the galleries were deprived of the thrill of seeing a crucial putt drop. And I don't think I would want to rob myself of that thrill either.

I've always enjoyed practicing putting. As a youngster I often stood on the practice green at the Virginia Park course in Johannesburg and said to myself: "Gary, you need this putt to win the British Open."

More times than not, I would "lose" the title, but when I did win the real thing at Muirfield in 1959, I felt certain the hundreds of hours I had devoted to putting were well worth the effort.

Many people have found putting on a carpet with a glass as the target hole improves their skill on the greens. This certainly helps a player develop a putting stroke that will put the ball on line.

However, putting is largely a matter of feel or touch, as opposed to brute, uncontrolled, and undirected force.

Therefore, putting into a glass does little to help a golfer develop the ability to hit the ball the correct distance—and this is where feel is important. I have found it better to putt from varying distances to a chalk mark, or—if your wife objects—a piece of string stretched across the rug. By stroking the ball to reach the string you develop feel that will carry over onto the regular greens, even if the texture is far different from that of your carpeting.

Like many players, including my friendly rival Arnold Palmer, I remove my glove before putting in order to give my hands more feel for the shot.

Putting is a three-phased operation. To be consistently successful you must have (1) the ability to pick the correct line, (2) the ability to stroke the ball along that line, and (3) the proper mental attitude. Without all three no golfer can be outstanding on the greens.

Of these three requisites, the ability to select the correct line—to read the green—is most constant. Stroking the ball properly and maintaining a proper mental outlook can vary, depending on your physical makeup at the time.

But once developed, skill in reading greens becomes habit, a routine as easily controlled as deciding what clothes to wear each morning.

Just as a well-dressed man concerns himself with details —the cut of his suit, the knot in his tie, or the shine on his shoes—the successful putter considers all details when picking the line for his putt.

People often ask me what I'm looking for when I sometimes peer into the hole before I putt. Believe it or not, the hole can be a big help in deciding which way a ball will roll as it nears the hole. And this is the most important phase of a putt, because near the cup it lessens in speed and therefore becomes more susceptible to variations in the green.

Peeking in the cup tells me many things. First, I note the depth of soil that appears above the metal cup. If there is a deeper layer of soil above one side of the cup than the other, I know that the putt will break—at least when it nears the cup—to the side with less topsoil.

This is true because greenskeepers set the cups as near upright as possible so the flagstick will not lean. If the green's surface is not level, there obviously will be more soil showing above the upright cup on the hole's high side than on the side to which the green slopes.

I also notice the grass around the edge of the hole. If

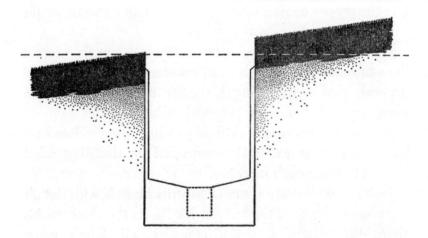

Amount of topsoil above the cup can tell golfer how putt will break. If cup is planted vertically, more soil will appear above cup on high side of the hole than on low side.

there is more damage to the grass on one edge than on the other, chances are good that putts will roll to that side. Such damage is caused when balls bang against the low side of the hole. Naturally, on a slanted green putts will bounce against the low side of the hole with more force and frequency than against any other side.

On greens with grain (grass which lies flat instead of setting upright) the side of the cup toward which the grass lays will die more readily because the root system is severed on the "down-grain" side when the hole is cut.

Extreme grainy greens also take on a silvery sheen when you look in the same direction the grain runs. This sheen is caused by mowers clipping the fibrous runners of the grass. The green will contain patches of dark green grass as you look into the grain from the opposite direction.

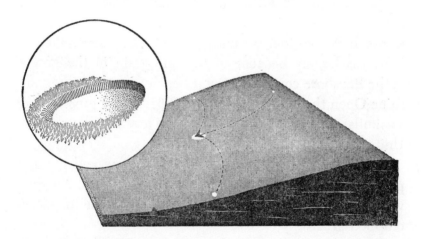

Damage to edge of cup (see inset) is most likely to appear on low or down-grain side of hole. Thus cup damage is a clue to direction putt will break on a slanted or grainy green.

Remember that your putts will run much faster with the grain and much slower against it. Cross-grain putts will break with the grain just as if you were putting on a side-hill slope.

You know, of course, it is illegal to roughen the grass on a green to determine which way the grass lays. Invariably, however, the grass just off a green on the fringe will lay in the same direction as the green itself. And it is legal to brush your putter across the fringe, thus determining the direction of grain.

Golfers on the American tour are quite conscious of grain on greens they play, but I'll tell you that grain in America cannot begin to compare with the "knap," as we call it, on South African courses. Our courses at home are the most difficult in the world to putt, simply because of the grain. South African grain usually grows toward the direction the sun rises, and it can take a level 12-foot putt as much as two feet off line.

It was largely because of extreme grain in the greens at the Bayshore course in Miami Beach that I won the Sunshine Open there in the spring of 1961. Those greens were as similar to South African greens as any I've seen in the United States.

In addition to allowing for a green's slope and grain, a player should also be conscious of wind direction. A strong wind will affect your putt, especially on "slick" or close-cropped greens.

To determine the line of a putt, I look it over from all angles. This means not only from behind the ball, but also from behind the cup and from the sides. I note not only the side roll, but also the degree of upward or downward slope between the ball and the hole.

I realize this takes time *and golf today is already played much too slowly by the average player.* However, I feel it is important to consider all details in determining your putting line. Much of your preparation can take place while others are putting, thereby saving time. Move while they are between shots and be ready to go when it's your turn.

When I play for a putt to break, say from left to right, and my ball finishes below the cup to the right, it amuses me to have someone from the gallery come up and say, in effect:

"What happened? Surely you could see that putt would break to the right."

Certainly I saw the break. But what my friend from the gallery forgot was that it's one thing to read a putt correctly, and another to putt it along the intended line.

That leads us into the second phase of putting—the mechanics of the stroke.

Putting mechanics vary with the individual and many great putters have used many different styles.

Bobby Locke, whom I regard as the finest putter I've ever seen, uses a great deal of wrist action. He takes the club back well inside his intended line and then loops it back squarely to the ball. He even moves his body during the stroke. This would mean sure trouble for most players.

On the other hand, there are great putters who use little, if any, wrist action. Art Wall is one who putts very successfully with what is largely a stiff-wristed movement. I've read where Bobby Jones had a smooth, flowing putting action, but many great putters of today, like Billy Casper and Doug Ford, make a quick, short stab at the ball.

To me the most natural putting method is to use a short,

but rhythmical tapping movement on short putts, and a more wristy, flowing stroke on longer ones.

I have never known a great putter who took his putter outside the intended line on his backswing. This causes you to either cut across the ball so that it rolls to the right of target, or to pull it to the left with a slightly closed face. A consistent putter must take the putter head straight back from the target line or slightly inside. If the latter is the case, one must still return the putter to the ball along this line. Keeping your right elbow against your side, except on very long putts, will help guard against moving the putter head outside the target line.

Despite Bobby Locke's style, I feel the majority of golfers cannot putt well day after day and still move their head or body during the stroke. Head movement destroys rhythm and timing. I've seen countless short putts missed in pro-amateur tournaments by amateur golfers who fail to keep their heads motionless and see that putter actually strike the ball.

It is important to keep the putter head low to the ground on the backswing, but it is even more important to keep it low on the follow through. This will help prevent lifting your head before the putter contacts the ball. If you learn nothing else from this chapter, you should remember to keep your head and body still during the putting stroke.

Also, I feel it is important to address the putt with your eyes directly over the ball so that you can sight the shot directly down the line. To me, putting with the eyes in any other position is as senseless as shooting a gun while holding it out to one side instead of looking through the sights.

I don't like to advocate any specific putting grip. There

are many which are suitable. Whatever feels comfortable to you should be the best as far as you are concerned.

Personally, I use the reverse overlap grip with both thumbs down the top of the club shaft. This grip has the forefinger of my left hand lapping over the fingers of my right. It gives me a feeling of togetherness between my hands, and this is good because I want them to work as a unit. I also get a feeling of unity in the grip by having my palms face each other. The back of my left hand and the palm of my right face the intended line throughout the stroke.

I keep my weight on my left foot—specifically my left heel—during the putt. This helps eliminate any tendency to move my body during the stroke.

On straight-in putts I play the ball opposite my front toe. On putts that will roll to the left, either because of slope or cross-grain, I play the ball back a bit in my stance. This keeps my hands ahead of the ball so that the putt will not veer to the left at the start. For putts that break to the right I play the ball just outside my left toe—farther forward than normal—to keep my hands from getting ahead of the ball and possibly pushing it to the right.

Like Sam Snead and other American professionals, I have also found it helps to putt over a spot near the ball. After I have chosen my line to the hole, I pick a blade of grass on that line and about two feet from the ball. Then I try to putt over that spot. If my line to the hole is correct and if I stroke the ball on this line for the first two feet with the right amount of force, I've done all I can to make it drop.

I am often asked which type of putter is best. In the

past I've replied without hesitation that I prefer the center-shafted variety. I've leaned recently, however, toward the mallet-type putter. It was with this putter that I won the Masters and I find it performs very well on all types of greens.

If you are like me, you no doubt have discovered that another try at a putt you have already missed invariably drops into the hole. This results partly because your first putt gave you the correct line. But I also think the second try is usually more successful because you are more relaxed. That brings us to the third phase of successful putting—the proper mental attitude.

I can't offer a sure-fire cure for the "yips," what Americans call tension, during putting. If I could I'm sure that Ben Hogan, still one of the greatest players from tee to green, would put me on his payroll immediately.

However, I do feel most people "yip" putts because they are afraid of missing them.

The best outlook on putts is to say to yourself, "I'm going to give this putt the best stroke I can, and if it goes in, it goes in."

Try to block all thoughts of missing out of your mind. Instead, visualize how the ball will look dropping into the cup.

Then be sure that you do not lift your head to watch the ball until it is well on its way.

Believe me, the odds on making a five-footer are in your favor. Outside that distance, I don't know. All you can do is to stroke it properly and hope.

On the tour we play on a wide variety of greens. When I won the Masters I putted very well over beautiful greens. Then in my next tournament, the Houston Classic, I putted on public course greens that had been subject to heavy play and were not as true as those at Augusta.

I made the mistake of worrying about missing putts because of the rough greens. This negative attitude soon affected my putting stroke and my confidence. Bad putting cost me many dollars in the weeks following, especially in the U. S. Open at Oakland Hills, where I hit the ball for 72 holes as well as I ever have at any time in my life but still only finished in a tie for ninth place.

Poor putting can sap your confidence and affect the rest of your game. After you miss a few short birdie putts, it is natural that you develop a "what's the use" attitude on your shots to the green.

That's why putting practice is so important, and why my putting partner Fardel Allem has been such a help to me.

PUTTING CHECKPOINTS

- ✔ The successful putter considers all details when selecting the line for his putt.

- ✔ Putts will run faster with the grain; slower against. Cross-grain putts will break with the grain just as on a sidehill slope.

- ✔ Never take your putter outside the intended line on the backswing.

- ✔ Never move your head or body during the stroke.

✔ It is important to keep the putter head low on the back-swing, but even more important to keep it low on the follow through.

✔ Address the putt with your eyes directly over the ball.

✔ Give every putt the best stroke possible. Don't worry about missing.

✔ Do not lift your head until the ball is well on its way.

CHAPTER 5

WHEN IN TROUBLE

I WAS playing in a London tournament a few years back and needed a five on the last hole to tie for the title. My second shot veered off line and the ball came to rest almost against a wall near the green. Rather than play a conventional shot away from the wall and then chipping for a chance at one putt, I decided to be fancy.

I intentionally banged the shot at the wall, hoping the ball would bounce off and onto the green.

It came off the wall in fine shape, but instead of finishing on the green it ricocheted back and hit me in the cheek. The force of the blow actually knocked me cold, momentarily.

Finally, I regained my senses—at least a portion of them. Still groggy, I chipped onto the green and somehow knocked a long putt into the hole.

I thought I had tied for the lead. Then officials informed me I had been penalized for "interfering" with the flight of my shot off the wall. I had lost the tournament.

Looking back on this incident, I think that under similar

circumstances I would again play the shot off the wall. If it had finished on the green, I would have had a putt to win.

There are times in golf when it is necessary to gamble. Usually, however, when you face a trouble shot from sand, rough, or water the best thing to do is to accept your problem. Don't try for a miracle shot, unless you need one to win.

The best thing to say about trouble shots is that the word "trouble" describes the situation perfectly. Your first concern should be to escape. If you are lucky or skillful, you may still get your par.

Failure to heed this advice cost me the Transvaal Open title some years back.

Leading Bobby Locke by one stroke after three rounds, I was paired with him on the final 18. I hooked my drive on the first hole into trees on the left. The ball bounced farther left, well away from the trees but still in the rough.

My safest route to the green was down the adjoining fairway on the left and then over the trees and onto the green with a wedge shot. Chances were good that I would have bogeyed the hole with a five. There was also a chance I might have dropped a putt for a par.

But being a bit flustered—and this often happens when a shot finishes in the rough—I decided to gamble. I tried to hit a 4-wood over the trees and onto the green from a fairly bad lie. Instead, my ball caught the trees again. I finally finished with a seven on the hole. Bobby got his par and I was out of the lead for the rest of the tournament. He finally beat me by three strokes.

Had I accepted the penalty for missing the tee shot and played safe with my second, it is likely I could have finished this hole with no less than a bogey and I would have been tied with Locke. Instead I handed him a two-shot lead.

I'll say it again! ALWAYS TAKE THE SHORTEST ROUTE OUT OF TROUBLE, at least, most of the time.

The trouble shot that gives me the least trouble is hitting from sand. This isn't as easy a shot as some people would have you believe. But I do think a golfer can become proficient on sand shots if he will invest in a sand wedge, a half-hour lesson with his pro, and some practice time.

When I first started golf, my family stayed at a house on a course in Johannesburg. I had a big bag of practice balls and I would pitch shots from alongside the house into a nearby sand trap. Then I'd go over to the trap and hit the balls from there—regardless of how they lay in the sand—onto a green.

That way I learned to hit sand shots from all different kinds of lies. Today, largely as a result of this practice, I can honestly say the blast from sand is my best shot in golf.

In winning the British Open in 1959 and the Masters in 1961, I found myself in sand traps a total of 17 times. I managed to get down in two—one sand shot and one putt—on 13 occasions.

The person who has a sand wedge—the blaster—for these shots has a distinct advantage. This club, with its heavy head and thick, rounded sole or flange on the bottom, readily slides under a ball in the sand without cutting too deep. A 9-iron with its lighter head and sharper cutting edge tends to dig and stick in the sand. Thus the 9-iron loses too much clubhead speed and your shot may fail to reach the green.

The blaster has a dual purpose. It is also useful when

you have a good lie in the fairway and need a high soft
shot over trees or a bunker.

The first thing I do on a bunker (or trap) shot is to test
the texture of the sand. Not with your club—you are not
allowed to ground your club in the sand. However, you
can get a pretty good idea of depth and consistency by
working your shoes into the sand. This also gives you a
good footing for the shot. If you fail to take a firm footing
beforehand, you may slide during the swing and almost
automatically hit a bad shot.

I address the sand shot with a slightly open stance—that
is with my left foot pulled farther back from the target
line. I also keep the toes of both shoes pointed slightly
toward the target.

I position myself so the ball is opposite my left foot. This
is important in order to have the clubhead slide under the
ball.

I keep most of my weight on my left foot, both at address and throughout the swing. Also, I address the ball
with the clubface slightly open, or turned to the right of
target.

I aim for a spot about two inches behind the ball, where
I want the clubhead to enter the sand.

I swing largely with hands and arms—using very little
body and leg movement, only enough to give me a feeling
of rhythm.

Because of the open stance, my backswing automatically
takes the clubhead a bit outside the target line. An outside-in downswing results, and with the open clubface, it
helps the clubhead slide under the ball and through the
sand without digging too deeply.

Because my weight remains forward on the left foot, my

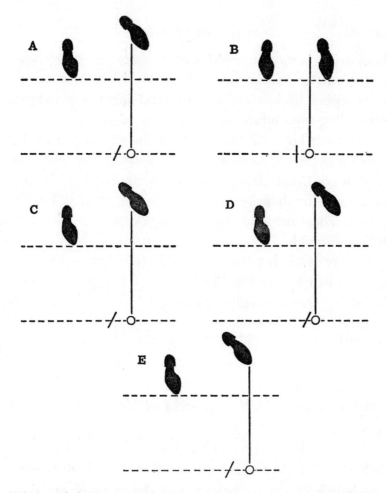

A) Basic sand shot—stance is open, left foot facing target considerably and right slightly. Ball is played off left foot. Club face is opened to the right and enters sand about 2" behind ball.

B) Buried lie in sand—stance is square with only left foot pointed slightly toward target. Ball played farther back in stance with clubface square. Club again enters sand about 2" behind ball.

C) Shot from wet sand—same stance and ball placement as for basic sand shot, and clubface opened to right. Only difference is that club enters sand farther behind ball —about 3 inches—because it will not cut as deeply in wet sand.

D) Uphill shot in sand—same as basic shot except that ball played a bit farther back in stance—note line going to left heel—and club enters sand closer to ball—about 1" from it—player must be extra sure to move club through sand on this shot since it must cut through more sand.

E) Downhill in sand—same as basic except ball played even farther forward in stance —note line going to toe—and club to enter sand farther behind ball—about three inches, depending on incline of slope.

backswing is more upright and includes an early cocking of the wrists. This keeps me from touching the sand with a sweeping backswing, which could incur a penalty for grounding my club.

The most important thing about the explosion shot is to make sure the clubhead accelerates through the sand. Most people are timid about explosion shots, anyway. It seems unnatural for them to take a full swing from just off the green. Therefore you must train yourself to take a full follow through.

On my sand shot from alongside the 18th green at Augusta when I won the Masters, all I thought about was following through with my swing. That's why I was able to put the ball close enough to the hole to sink my putt for the title.

One thing that bothers most golfers with sand shots is judging how far the ball will fly. This is something a golfer must learn for himself. A lot depends on the texture of the sand.

As I mentioned, I try to hit about two inches behind the ball on most sand shots. I control the shot's distance by the length of my backswing and the force of my downswing. When I'm a great distance from the green, I might try to contact the sand about one inch behind the ball. *But normally I'd say two inches is about right.*

When the ball is buried in the sand, I follow the same procedure as with a normal sand shot, with three exceptions:

First, my clubface is square to, or facing, the target at address, rather than slightly open. This helps the clubhead cut deeper and under the buried ball.

Second, I swing more upright than normal so that my club enters the sand with more of a downward blow. Again, my weight is on the left foot.

Third, I allow for the ball to roll a greater distance on the green than it would from a level lie. Because my club cuts deeper into the sand it imparts less backspin on the ball.

Again, I bring the club through the sand with a full follow through.

I never, never chip from sand. The odds are too great that with a short chip swing you will hit behind the ball and not get the club through the sand. I've watched many great players try to chip out of sand and leave the ball in the bunker. Rarely does a proficient sand player leave a blast shot in the trap.

If you do prefer to chip from sand, make sure you keep your weight forward on the left foot throughout the swing. Play the ball as you would on a normal chip shot, concentrating on hitting the ball before your club contacts the sand. You must have an outstanding lie in the trap before you can chip.

Personally, I don't think I've ever putted out of sand. But I will say it is all right for weekend players, providing the sand is firm, the ball is setting up, and there is no lip on the trap.

In blasting from wet sand, I try to hit a bit farther behind the ball than normal. I know my clubhead will not cut so deeply in wet sand. My shot might fly over the green unless I slow the clubhead speed by hitting farther behind the ball.

When I have an uphill lie in sand, I realize the ball will fly almost straight up and will finish short of the target unless I contact the sand closer to the ball than normal—I'd say about one inch sway.

On downhill lies I hit the sand about three inches behind the ball with a sharp downward blow so that the club will cut under, rather than into the ball.

From fairway traps my first concern is merely to get out. I make certain to select a club with enough loft to clear the bunker edge. I position myself as I would on a normal fairway shot with the club I have selected. But I do take a wider stance than normal in order to minimize body movement and weight shifting during the swing. Again my weight is forward and I make sure to contact the ball first. I like to feel that I'm sort of flicking the ball out with my hands.

If I have a good lie in a fairway bunker with no lip blocking the line, I might try a wood shot. Here I play the ball well forward in my stance and concentrate on a square club-ball contact.

Success on sand shots is simply a matter of sound technique and practice. Many weekend players could lower their scores considerably if they learned the technique, preferably first-hand in a lesson from a professional.

But, as in any other phase of golf, practice is the key to sand shot success.

Once Jerry Barber, a great sand player, was practicing bunker shots. He hit one ball near the flag. The next shot went in.

A person watching Jerry told him:

"Gee, you sure are a lucky trap shot player."

"Yes, I know," Jerry replied. "And the harder I practice, the luckier I get."

This is something I feel very strongly about: there are

a lot of rules penalizing the golfer for infractions. I think there should be a rule penalizing the golfer—man or woman —who doesn't cover the marks they make in the sand.

There is nothing worse than to find your ball in a hole in the trap, just because some jerk did not take the time to smooth out his footprints or repair his damage.

Another common trouble shot facing the golfer is when he hits his ball into the rough. One thing many golfers fail to realize is that a ball will react differently from a shot out of the rough than from the fairway.

A ball hit out from the rough has a tendency to take less backspin because a great deal of grass intervenes between club and ball at impact. The ball will run like a scalded cat.

Therefore, when shooting out of rough, it is wise to use a more lofted club than for a shot of the same distance from fairway. If I have a shot that would normally take a 4-iron, I probably will use a 5-iron playing from the rough.

This is a general rule, however. Sometimes you will encounter rough so thick that only a wedge will cut through the grass.

Such was the case in the 1958 U.S. Open at Southern Hills Country Club in Tulsa, Okla. I had 287 there for 72 holes and thought I had done a masterful job. Tommy Bolt's winning score of 283 was one of the most remarkable showings I've ever witnessed on a golf course.

On shots from rough I grip tighter than normal with my left hand. This helps me get the club through the grass without the shaft turning in my hand.

When swinging a highly lofted club, say from a 7-iron through a wedge, I keep most of my weight on my left foot. With a less lofted club than a 7-iron, I use the normal weight distribution as for a fairway shot.

A most important fundamental of shots from rough is to contact the ball before hitting the turf. You should meet the ball with a sharply descending clubhead. An upright backswing, with the wrists breaking early, will help achieve this downward hit.

Hitting the ball with a downward motion, as opposed to sweeping it away, is necessary to keep the amount of grass between the clubhead and ball at a minimum. This provides a more solid club-ball contact with less chance of having the club turn in the grass. Also, an upright backswing reduces the chance of stubbing your clubhead on the takeaway.

I must admit the golfer who is physically strong has a big advantage in playing out of rough. Players like Mike Souchak and George Bayer excel for this reason.

But in the final analysis it is clubhead speed which makes the difference. Therefore, even a smaller player who generates great clubhead speed can do well out of rough. Ben Hogan, though certainly not a physical giant, has impressed me with the way he plays out of the tall grass.

In addition to mastering play from sand and rough, the finished golfer also knows how to hook or slice intentionally around obstacles such as trees.

To hook intentionally I merely grip the club with my hands turned a bit farther to the right than normal. I address the ball with my right foot pulled back farther than the left from the target line in a closed stance position. I take the clubhead back well inside the target line on the backswing and then roll my right hand over my left in the hitting area.

To hit a slight hook, or "draw," I follow the same procedure, except that I do not modify my grip.

To slice I turn my hands a bit more to the left than normal on the club. I open my stance by pulling my left foot farther back from the target line than my right. Also, I take the clubhead back slightly outside the target line. Finally, I try to have my hands well ahead of the clubhead at impact.

I follow the same procedure to hit a fade, or modified slice, except that I do not alter my grip.

I must admit I haven't had much experience in hitting out of water. Yet, occasionally in the heat of competition you might be forced to give it a go.

I would treat the water shot much as I do an explosion shot from sand. However, keep your clubface square to the target line, rather than slightly open. Also employ a square, rather than open, stance.

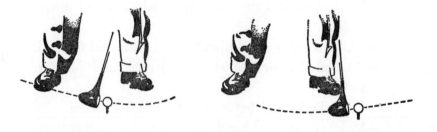

In the drawing at the left we are shown how to play the ball when hitting into the wind in order to keep the shot low. Ball is played back in stance so that clubhead meets ball when it is still traveling slightly on the downswing. This reduces club's loft so that shot goes low.

Drawing at right shows how to play shot with the wind. Ball is played farther forward so that club-ball contact is made when clubhead is starting up on follow through. Thus loft is increased and higher shot results.

Again, hit about two inches behind the ball because your clubhead will skid forward in the water.

I wouldn't advise trying a shot from water that is more than two inches deep. In water any deeper than that the chances are good that your clubhead will never reach the ball. At best you'll get a thin hit—and a fat score.

TROUBLE SHOT CHECKPOINTS

✔ When in trouble, your first thought should be to escape. Don't try for a miracle shot, unless you need one to win.

✔ Sand explosion technique:
—Address ball with slightly open stance, toes pointed slightly toward target.
—Play ball opposite left foot.
—Clubface opened to right of target at address.
—Most of weight on left foot at address and during swing.
—Club to enter sand about two inches behind ball.
—Control distance of shot by length and force of swing.
—Little body and leg movement during swing.
—Make certain clubhead accelerates into and through sand.

✔ Hitting from rough:
—Use more lofted club than normal to allow for additional roll.
—Grip tighter than normal with left hand.
—Keep weight on left foot for shot with highly lofted clubs.
—Contact ball before turf with a downward blow.

CHAPTER 6

WEATHERING THE STORM

DURING MY many world tours, people around the globe have asked me the same question:

"What makes golf such an intriguing game?"

In answering, I tell them the game has such a hold on golfers because they compete not only against an opponent, but also against the course, against par, and most surely— against themselves. Anyone who conquers these four formidable foes derives a great deal of satisfaction, and it is that satisfaction which makes golf irresistible to me.

But as I write this chapter it occurs to me that on some days the golfer actually finds himself doing battle with a fifth dimension—the weather. Sometimes this foe is the most difficult to defeat.

Going into the final round of the 1961 Lucky International tournament at San Francisco's Harding Park course, I found myself four strokes out of the lead, tied for seventh place with such fine players as Ken Venturi, Arnold Palmer, Don January and Jay Hebert. Still, the night before the final 18 I felt confident I could win and even passed on this sentiment to some friends with whom I had dinner.

The next day it rained as I've seldom seen it rain before. As singer Bing Crosby once remarked: "I was putting against the tide all the way."

That day I played one of my finest rounds to shoot a 65 and win the $9,000 first prize by two strokes.

During the round I kept telling myself that I wasn't the only man on the island. It was just as wet for everyone else as for me.

That's the only attitude to take when playing golf in bad weather. Just keep plugging along trying to make every shot the best possible. If you hit a bad shot or get a bad break, remember that the same thing could be happening to everyone else.

More strokes have been lost to par in bad weather because of improper attitude—blaming the weather; feeling sorry for oneself; giving up; etc.—than were ever lost because of the weather itself.

I cannot guarantee a method for anyone to attain the proper attitude for bad weather golf. That has to come from the individual himself. But I can suggest ways to prepare for, and play in, wind, rain and extreme heat or cold. Let us first discuss playing in the wind.

I find the American pros to be the world's best players in just about every aspect of golf. However, I do feel most of them are poor wind players in comparison with their other abilities.

There are a few good wind players in America—Palmer, Venturi, Bob Rosburg and most of the Texas boys like January, Ernie Vossler, and Billy Maxwell. But the majority are not too good.

Seldom do I see an American pro, when playing into the wind, take more club than he needs. If he needs a 6-iron to reach the green, he hits a 6-iron. When I'm playing into the wind and need a 6-iron, I hit a 4-iron, gripping the club well down the shaft.

This gives me the low shot I want into the wind, without having to consciously change my swing. The less lofted club provides the low shot, and shortening my grip makes the 4-iron travel about the same distance as a normal 6-iron.

In most cases I think it's a bad practice to alter your swing to provide for a shot low into the wind. It's tough enough merely to keep a golf shot straight. But by hitting more club with a shortened grip, you don't have to try to hit it low. It just happens.

Also, you should never try to hit the ball with more force than normal. It's better to use more club and concentrate on taking the club back slowly from the ball for the first foot of the backswing. Then just swing through smoothly.

If anything, when playing into a strong wind, it's better to shorten the backswing more than normal. This will make the swing more compact and give better club control. Also, it will supply better balance throughout.

I find that to hit a low tee shot with a driver, it's best to address the ball a bit farther back, toward the center of my stance. This not only keeps my drives low, but also gives them a bit of a hook, which is desirable against the wind because the ball will shoot out and run farther than normal.

You don't want to slice, or even fade, into a headwind. A high-rising shot will expend itself too quickly in the wind.

When playing in a crosswind, many golfers make the mistake of trying to compensate for the wind by cutting the shot into it. Few players are strong enough to slice a ball into a right-to-left wind and still get the distance necessary on the shot.

Don't fight the wind—use it. When it's blowing from right to left, aim to the right and let the wind blow your ball back to the middle of the fairway. Aim left when the wind is left to right.

When I'm driving with the wind, I try to hit the ball high. I do this by positioning it a bit farther forward in my stance than normal. Thus, I hit the ball more toward the upswing. Sometimes in a strong wind I can hit a 2-wood as far as I can a driver because the brassie, with its additional loft, gets the ball higher in flight.

When hitting with the wind to a green, I prefer to keep the ball low. I find it easier to judge how far a low shot

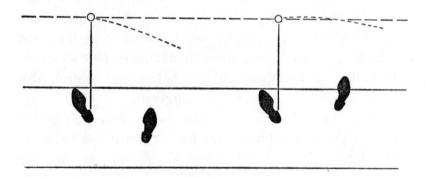

Drawing on left shows stance and path of clubhead on backswing when playing a slight intentional hook—or draw. Note stance closed with left toe pointed out more than right. Club goes back more or less on same angle as feet are positioned, or well inside target line. When club returns to ball on this path it puts a right-to-left or hook spin on the ball.

Drawing on right shows same things but for a slight intentional slice or fade. Note open stance and club's path going slightly outside target line at start of backswing. If it returns to ball on this path a left-to-right or slice spin will be placed on the ball.

will roll with the wind than to determine how far a high shot will fly. You don't know how strong the air currents are up there, and the ball might fly well over the green. Also, a strong tailwind tends to reduce backspin on the ball.

So, on with-the-wind shots to a green, I position the ball back farther in my stance than normal so that my hands lead the clubhead into the ball with a downward blow. I try to hit the ball first before contacting the turf.

An exception is when I must clear a hazard in front of the green on a downwind shot. Naturally, a low shot will either fall short and roll into the hazard, or carry it and roll over the green.

It's a delicate shot and requires carrying the hazard with as much backspin on the ball as I can apply.

I address the ball for such a shot with a slightly open stance—left foot pulled back farther than the right from the target line—and with the clubface opened a bit to the right. This gives me a slightly outside-in swing which adds "bite" to the shot.

When playing in wet weather, there are many things you can do before hitting the ball to give you an advantage over most amateur golfers.

For instance, I see many golfers in the rain who carry a towel on their bag or let their caddie carry one. This is not nearly so effective as hanging the towel from one of the ribs on the underside of your umbrella. There it will stay much drier.

I always use the towel to dry my hands and the club both before and after each shot. If I take a practice swing, I dry the clubhead again before the actual shot. For good shot control the clubface should be as dry as possible.

It is important your glove remain dry, too. I carry three or four old gloves in my bag as substitutes for such a condition.

I also make certain my spikes are free from debris before each shot. Balance during the swing is important, especially in wet weather.

The next time you go into a locker room, notice the number of golf shoes that have worn-down spikes. If people realized the number of strokes they could save by spending a dollar or so to have their shoes respiked, they would save themselves a lot of frustration when playing on wet turf.

Shot planning is an important phase of golf, even under normal weather conditions. In wet weather it becomes doubly significant.

When sand traps are wet, your chances of encountering a plugged (buried) lie increase. When the rough is wet, your ball will slide all over the clubface, and it is difficult to make the clubhead cut.

Therefore, I'm extra careful to plan beforehand just what type of shot I want to hit and where I want it to land. I do this planning while I'm still under the umbrella. On tee shots I instruct the caddie to stand over me with the umbrella while I tee the ball.

Normally I prefer to hit a low-flying ball, but when playing in wet weather I try to hit my shots high. Naturally a low shot will not go very far on a soggy fairway, so there is no advantage in playing for a roll.

Therefore I play all of my shots off the left heel. I try to keep my body behind the ball throughout the swing and to bring my right shoulder well under on the downswing.

All of this helps me hit my shots cleanly off the turf. I

try not to hit down on the ball with irons, as I would on dry fairways. I want to keep my clubhead from cutting into soggy turf for fear that it will cut too deep and cause the shot to fall short of the target.

As when playing in the wind, I find it helpful to take a slow, short backswing on shots from soggy turf. This minimizes the chance of slipping and provides a firm balance throughout the swing.

The short backswing, if smooth and rhythmical, also enables me to hit the ball squarely. If there is one thing not to do on soggy fairways, it's to let the clubhead hit behind the ball and bury in the turf. Hit the ball as cleanly as possible and then allow the swing a long follow through.

The most important thing about playing in extremely cold weather is to keep the body and hands as warm as possible.

I wear wool trousers and long underwear in cold weather. Also I feel a woolen turtle-neck shirt and a cashmere sweater are ideal. I know cashmere sweaters are a bit on the expensive side for the average person but they are ideal for cold weather golf, especially if it is also wet. They are soft and supple and offer great protection against the rain.

A good way to keep your hands warm is to bend your fingers back. Also, flicking your fingers before each shot helps the blood circulate. Then rub them together.

My favorite golfing weather comes during the summer months when the sun really beats down. I like to perspire freely when I play because this makes my swing smooth and supple. You will notice that most of the really low scores are shot in very hot weather.

However, too much heat can be an evil. I find it helps

to drink a great deal of liquid during a round. I make certain my caddie carries a towel that is moist on one end so I can wipe my brow occasionally and yet dry my hands before every shot.

Everyone should wear a golf cap in extreme heat, not only as an aid to their golf, but also as a safeguard against heat prostration.

I have also found that wearing white clothes is a big help in very hot weather because white reflects the sun's rays, whereas dark clothing tends to attract heat.

No matter what the weather, your golf game will be no better than your mental attitude. In bad weather, with the wind and the rain in your face, it is doubly difficult to come back after a bad hole.

Just remember Walter Hagen's sage observation that any golfer, no matter how well he plays, can expect to have at least four bad shots a round.

I'd add to Mr. Hagen's comment that even if you hit 40 bad shots you should still keep trying.

The other fellow might have missed 41.

BAD WEATHER CHECKPOINTS

✔ Try to disregard bad shots or bad breaks. Other players are suffering the same fate.

✔ In windy weather:
    —Hit tee shots low into the wind by playing ball back in stance.
    —Hit tee shots high with the wind by playing ball forward, teeing it high.
    —Keep shots to the green low, regardless of wind

direction. Play ball well back in stance, contact it with downward blow.

—Use more club than necessary into a headwind. Use a full, firm swing but shorten grip to minimize distance.

—Don't fight a cross-wind by hooking or slicing into it.

✔ In wet weather:

—Study each shot carefully before leaving the protection of an umbrella.

—Play all shots off the left heel to obtain maximum flight.

—Pick shots cleanly from grass so the club will not cut into soggy turf.

✔ A slow, short backswing is helpful in maintaining balance and footing in both wind and rain.

Gary exudes determination following a tee shot enroute to 1961 Masters triumph.

Another putt in Gary Player's successful drive toward the 1961 Masters.

Player works out of the thick English rough in the British Open

In a drizzling rain Player hits from a sand trap to the second green during first round of The Masters Golf Tournament in 1961.

Rooting a putt home

Above, you see three top women professionals, Ruth Jessen (top three photos), Betsy Rawls (middle photos) and Jo Ann Prentice (bottom row) show swing features that Player advocates. Note that each addresses ball with knees and back slightly bent. All take club back in a wide arc with delayed wrist cocking and no body sway. All display maximum coiling of shoulders and hips.

Player demonstrates the 5-iron.

Gary's tournament and exhibition schedule takes him all over the world. Here he is embarking on a transatlantic jet with his wife, Vivienne.

CHAPTER 7

PLAYING YOUR BEST
IN COMPETITION

The Augusta National course, where the Masters tournament is held annually, reminds me of a mouse trap with a piece of cheese in the middle. If you get too greedy the trap will crush you.

This comparison occurred to me the night before the 1961 Masters as I sat in the panelled family room of the private home where my family and I stayed in Augusta. My tee time was several hours ahead, but already I was competing, in a sense.

As I had done so often in the past, I sat with a pencil and pad of paper and developed my plan.

I diagrammed certain holes, recording the placement of sand and water hazards. I noted which clubs I probably would use on these holes under various wind conditions. I charted certain holes where dangerous rough, hazards or terrain made it wise to avoid a certain side of a fairway or a green. I noted holes where I did not want to go over the green, and those where it was best not to be short. I also considered facts I had learned about certain greens during my practice rounds—where I might encounter grain, hidden rolls, and difficult pin positions.

These pre-tournament strategy sessions—especially before facing such a challenging course as the Augusta National—are just as important to me as the pre-examination cramming session to college students.

Reviewing the course not only gives me my plan, but also primes me mentally for the upcoming competition.

Any reader who plays competitive golf on unfamiliar courses, whether it be in interclub matches or a national tournament, would do well to indulge in such planning. It will give him that much advantage over his fellow-competitors.

My strategy sessions tell me which holes I can attack and which ones I should play defensively. I like to attack

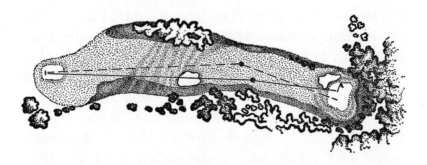

No. 1 (400-yds.). At Augusta, this was an "attacking" hole in Gary's Masters strategy. By driving over trap on right (solid line) he set himself up for birdies in three of the four rounds.

on all holes, but some that are extremely troublesome I must play conservatively.

In previous years I had started at Augusta by defending —just playing for pars. This time I decided to attack on the first hole. This hole is a 400-yard slight dogleg to the right with a large sand trap about 220 yards out on the right side of the fairway. I decided to have a full go at my drive; to hit it over the trap and as close to the green as possible.

I started with birdie threes on that hole on three of the four rounds, a tremendous start on that course. It gave me a terrific boost psychologically and possibly had some effect on other contenders who noted my birdies on the big scoreboards around the course that keep Masters galleries and competitors so well informed.

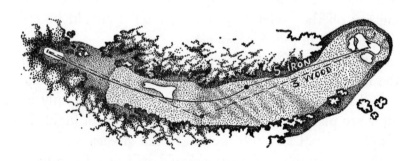

No. 2 (555-yds.). Also an attacking hole. By hooking his drive around the dogleg he took advantage of downhill roll and shortened second shot considerably.

The second hole, a 555-yard dogleg to the left, was also an attacking hole. During a practice round I had played a drive to the right, away from the trees on the left that blocked a direct route to the green. I found it required a 3-wood for me to reach that green.

Later I tried playing down the left side and hooking around the trees. The fairway slopes sharply toward the green on this side, providing additional distance, and I found I had only a 5-iron left. This green is well-guarded by traps so I felt it was worth the gamble off the tee to shorten my second shot by five clubs.

The 11th hole at Augusta is definitely a defensive hole. The green on this 445-yard test is partially tucked behind water on the left. Here, I don't even look at the flag while preparing for my second shot. I'm afraid I might get greedy and shoot directly for the hole.

Instead, I aimed about 40 yards to the right of the green to bring the ball in with a slight hook. The roll usually put me just off the green, from where I felt I should be able to get down in two for a par 4.

On the day of a tournament I find myself competing the minute I arrive at the course. Almost unconsciously I note wind and its direction and force. Wind not only can alter my plan because of its effect on a ball in flight, but also because of its tendency to dry the greens.

Of course, rain and extreme cold will also force me to alter my plan on some attacking holes, where I had counted on long tee shots. They may now become "play for par" holes because of conditions.

The wise golfer adds to his storehouse of knowledge about the course even during competition. Knowledge of

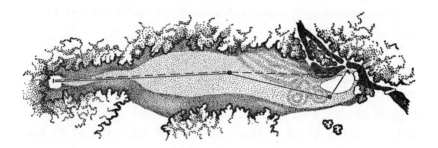

No. 11 (445-yds.). A defensive hole for Player in 1961 Masters. He played second shot
to right of green to avoid chance of catching water hazard that guards it on left front.

pin positions on upcoming holes is an important phase in
competing.

If someone in the gallery were to ask me after driving
on a hole where the pin was positioned, I'm sure that I
could tell him without glancing at the green. Most of the
time I could supply this information before I even arrive
at the tee.

Pin position determines largely where I will try to place
my drive. Most of the time I try to put my ball in a spot
that will give me an open shot to the flag.

Most courses are laid out so that I can note pin positions
on greens that are not to be played until several holes later.
This advance knowledge is invaluable because a pin position is often deceiving when viewed from the tee.

For instance, from the tee it may appear that a flag is positioned just behind and close to a trap. Thus, to avoid the trap, I might play my drive to the opposite side of the fairway, sacrificing some distance to provide a clear shot to the hole.

But when I approach that green, I discover that the flag is actually near the back of the green, well beyond the trap. Thus, I would realize too late that I could have played my tee shot directly toward the hole, gaining valuable yardage, because the trap offered little threat to an approach shot.

This advance knowledge of pin positioning played a big role in Art Wall's 1959 Masters victory when he birdied five of the last six holes.

Because the 18th green at Augusta is near the practice green, the first tee and the 10th tee, Art had ample opportunity that final day to determine beforehand that the flag on 18 was positioned up front, on the green's lower level.

Thus, when he played the hole he knew an approach shot which carried past the hole would leave him with a difficult downhill putt. So he placed his second shot about 12 feet short of the cup. He dropped the easier putt for a birdie three and won the title by one stroke.

Another big factor in competing successfully is the ability to control nervous tension. The jitters hit every golfer, from Hogan on down, sooner or later. They are nothing to be ashamed of. The most nervous I've ever been was on a golf course during the 1956 Ampol tournament in Australia.

Before the tournament I had promised my fiance, Vivienne Vervey, that if I won first prize of 5,000 pounds we would get married. We had been sweethearts a long time and wanted very much to become married.

Going into the final round I found myself leading by seven strokes. That day it rained and play was postponed 24 hours. The delay increased the tension, as I realized more and more how much top money would mean to Viv and myself.

Friends told me not to worry; that with a seven-shot lead I could hit a tennis ball around the course and still win. This sort of talk was well meant but only made me worry more. I knew that even an eight- or ten-stroke lead can vanish if some player gets hot and you play carelessly.

The next day my lead was still intact coming into the final holes. Yet, my nervous system was a mess. I actually thought I might faint from the pressure.

Then I did something that may help others in tense situations.

I bent over, as if to pick up some grass, and blew as much air as I could out of my lungs. Then I straightened up and inhaled the fresh air deeply. This eased my tension, and by continuing these breathing exercises I was able to finish the tournament on top.

Tension comes from fear of failure. In golf, jitters occur when you think about making a bad shot. You can bring on tension by thinking about catching a trap, hitting out of bounds, or missing a putt.

Positive thinking can help overcome such tension. If I'm inclined to feel nervous, I try to direct my thinking toward making a good shot. I visualize how a good shot will feel and look. Then I give it the best stroke or swing I can.

I must admit, however, that I would much rather feel a

bit tense on the day of a tournament than too relaxed. In some cases, the relaxed golfer is one who is stale—who has lost his edge. This is a common problem among pros on the American tour, where one can play in a tournament almost every week.

I have seen players become so sick of golf that it is a real effort for them to hit even one more shot. I think golfers like Sam Snead, Ben Hogan, Ted Kroll and Stan Leonard, who compete only occasionally on the tour, have a big advantage over others who play week after week. The occasional competitor is usually fresh—both mentally and physically. He is eager to compete.

Some days a golfer feels more like playing than on others, regardless of the number of rounds he has played in the recent past. I know on the fourth day of the 1961 Masters—the day when play was rained out—I didn't feel particularly charged up, even though I was in the lead, four strokes ahead of Arnold Palmer.

The next morning, after a day of rest, I was really eager to play. Even on the last nine when I started losing strokes to Palmer, I had a good mental outlook and kept giving every shot my best.

After winning the Masters, I experienced a terrific letdown and my game suffered considerably. Two weeks later at the Houston Classic I told some friends I was sick of golf. I made this remark in a moment of despair and certainly would have retracted it after some reflection. But it did show my attitude at the time.

When I feel stale, I try to find something that will increase my desire to compete. I would advise other golfers in a similar situation to do the same; that is, if they cannot forget golf for a while.

My big goal, the thing that keeps me from letting down in competition, is the desire to continue as the leading money-winner on the U.S. tour as I was in 1961. The $10,000 bonus it would mean from the First Flight company helps whet my desire to compete.

I am often asked about concentration in golf. Since this is a most important phase of competing, I think some comment is merited.

First, let me say no two golfers can put the same amount of concentration on the same things. Thus, it is impossible to tell someone how much they should apply themselves mentally to their game or what specific things they should stress.

Ben Hogan is a classic example of concentration, at least outwardly. Hogan gives the impression that his mind never wanders from the business at hand. I'm sure this is not actually the case, however. I don't think any man can apply himself to his game continuously for 18 holes. I think the game would lose all of its appeal in a short time for anyone who made it such a chore.

A golfer like Doug Sanders is the opposite extreme of Hogan. Doug has the ability to concentrate, but he applies it only when necessary. He can clown for the gallery, whistle, and occasionally back-hand a short putt into the hole. Like the great Walter Hagen, he can turn his concentration off or on at will.

I would guess that both Sanders and Hogan find their ability to concentrate varies from day to day. I know mine does.

Sometimes I realize I'm working too hard at my game. When this happens I find it helps to talk to the gallery or my playing partners, if I feel that conversation will not bother them. I often take time to look around me at the beauty of the scenery. In short, I try to enjoy myself and my golf and save intense concentration for the time when I feel it is needed.

At certain times I find my mind wandering too much from the game. When this happens I'll do anything to bring my attention back to golf and the situation of the moment. Sometimes a little thing like pacing off the distance of a tee shot will help return my thinking to the competition.

As I mentioned earlier, it is important to concentrate on the positive aspects of a situation. On each shot you should define your goals. Visualize the flight pattern your ball should take and imagine how your swing should feel to achieve such a flight. Recognize the problems of a shot situation, such as a close lie or an intervening hazard, and concentrate on overcoming the problems, not on the consequences of a bad shot.

Some people may have advised that you should not think about any specific thing in your swing, just on hitting the ball squarely. This is good advice, but I'm afraid a bit idealistic.

I know that when I'm playing well I'm usually thinking about two things during my swing. One is to shift my weight to my left foot immediately at the start of the downswing. The second subject of concentration varies from week to week, or day to day.

Anyone who has played much golf sooner or later develops the bogey habit. Bad holes seem to come in pairs or threes or fours for many golfers. I think in such cases the player's mental attitude has a great deal to do with his problem.

I condition myself against the bogey habit by realizing

before the round that I probably will hit at most 10 real good shots. I know that most PGA tournaments are won by a player who has suffered at least five bogies in 72 holes.

Thus when I get a pair of bogies back to back, I tell myself I can still win the tournament if I just start playing par golf.

The toughest thing for most people to learn in golf is to accept bad holes—and then forget about them.

Tommy Bolt is an example of a fine golfer who could be even better if he did not dwell on bad holes or bad breaks. At least, he gives that impression outwardly. On the other hand there are golfers like Doug Ford who can shrug off a bad hole and come back strongly.

I feel one of the qualities of a great golfer is to never give up, no matter how badly he may be scoring. When I see a player stand on the tee with a beautiful swing, I'm not overly impressed. What really impresses me is a player who is a good fighter. Arnold Palmer is a great fighter; he never gives up.

I can honestly say I have never let down or given up in a tournament. Many times I've been glad that I've forced myself to keep trying on every shot. It's surprising how many thousands of dollars I've made by not giving up. My victory in the Masters was a good example of this.

At one time in that final round I led Palmer by six strokes. Yet on the back nine I saw this lead vanish as I took a double-bogey seven on the 13th hole. Then I missed a short putt on the 15th and fell one shot behind.

Still, I managed to sink a 14-foot putt for a par on the 17th and a five-footer for a par after being trapped on 18.

Many people felt that I backed into the title when Palmer double-bogeyed the final hole. Since I also had a double-bogey, I prefer to think that I truly won the tournament with my putts on the final two holes.

Often, when the going gets tough, I find myself forcing my game by taking chances. Except when I need a fabulous shot to win the tournament, I try not to gamble unless the odds are in my favor.

The 15th hole at Augusta usually presents the problem of deciding whether or not to gamble. With water blocking the front of the green on this 520-yard hole, one must carefully consider his chances of reaching the target.

Here I will try to clear the water if I feel a well-hit shot with a 3-wood or less club will do the job. If I feel it would take a perfect shot, I will play short. Very seldom in golf do you hit a perfect shot.

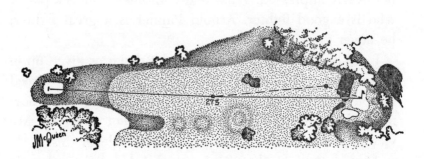

No. 15 (520-yds.). Forced Gary to decide whether or not to gamble on carrying water. Whenever a perfect shot was required to reach green, he played short of hazard.

So judgment in competition depends largely on the player's knowledge of his ability.

For example, a weight-lifter presses 100 pounds the first month. The next month he does 150. Then he gets greedy and tries to lift 300 pounds. He strains himself and never reaches the 300-lb. mark.

Golf is the same way. Don't force it. Remember about that mouse who went after the cheese.

CHECKPOINTS ON HOW TO COMPETE

✔ Analyze the course and develop a plan before the tournament. Decide which holes you will attack and which you will play for a par.

✔ Develop the habit of noting pin positions on upcoming holes.

✔ Deep breathing and positive concentration will help control the jitters.

✔ Concentration can be overdone. Enjoy yourself on the course and save the deep thinking for the important shots.

✔ Recognize shot problems, but think about overcoming them, not how they might hurt your shot.

✔ Learn to accept bad holes as being part of anyone's game and then forget about them.

✔ Never give up or let down.

✔ Take the gamble only when the odds are in your favor, or when you need a miracle shot to win the title.

CHAPTER 8

THE FINE ART
OF PRACTICING

MOST BABIES cannot walk for a year or so after birth. First they start crawling, then standing, walking and, finally, running. All these phases of infant development require experimentation, confidence and practice.

It's the same with golf.

A beginning golfer doesn't swing too well at first. Then he improves. In a year he should have a good swing. It's almost automatic if he has had sound instruction and has practiced the pro's advice.

Practice is the key to good golf. No man or woman can play to the best of his or her ability without it. You can read all the books and articles on golf that were ever printed, but you would be wasting your time if you didn't practice.

When I started golf, I headed for the practice tee about 8 o'clock in the morning. I'd hit balls until noon. Then I'd eat lunch and sleep until 2 P.M. Then I'd return to the course and practice until 6 P.M. I would work for hours on a single shot, such as the wedge, or an intentional hook or slice.

I lost 16 pounds my first year as a pro, largely from prolonged practice sessions.

Today I'm flattered when someone tells me my swing seems so natural. However, I chuckle to myself when I recall the hours and blistered hands that went into making it natural.

Successful practice is an art. There are some things you should do and others you should avoid.

Before my first trip overseas I often practiced in the rain, instead of sitting indoors sipping tea. I knew that in England I'd be doing a lot of playing in the rain, and I wanted to be familiar with the conditions.

However, unless it is absolutely necessary I feel it is unwise to practice in wet weather. You can develop bad habits such as forcing your swing, lunging at the ball, falling back on your right side and overpressuring your grip to control a wet club.

It is also difficult to maintain a smooth swing when practicing in the wind. However, wind can be an aid when you are working to cure certain faults.

For instance, I like to practice in a right to left wind if I'm trying to cure a hook. Such a wind forces me to guard against the hook. An opposite wind is ideal when working to cure a slice because it forces me to use more hand action to counteract the slice. If I've been hitting my shots too high, I like to practice hitting into the wind. This will force me to keep the ball low.

Always start your practice sessions with short shots. This not only gives you a good feel of the club and of rhythm in the swing, it also loosens the muscles.

Before the final round of the 1957 Canada Cup matches in Japan, my tee time drew near as I chatted with one of the players at the practice area. I heard someone calling my name to tee off. I hadn't hit a single practice shot.

I decided to hit four quick drives. In doing so I ricked my neck and had to play the entire round feeling pain on every full shot. Fortunately, I putted well and finished in a tie with Sam Snead and Dave Thomas of Wales for second place.

Ever since that experience I have made it a point to arrive early to give me plenty of time to hit shots before playing.

Now, before a round I hit six wedge shots and three shots each with the 7, 5 and 3-irons. Then I hit three 4-woods, three spoon shots and four drives. Finally I practice my chipping and putting.

This last phase of pre-round practice is very important. After hitting full wood shots, I must putt and chip to regain the feel for the short shots. Sometime, you ought to hit a bag of balls with your driver. Then try dropping a half-wedge shot on a target. You'll see what I mean when I say that practicing full shots can destroy your touch, at least temporarily.

Also, never rush your practice. Nothing can ruin the tempo of your swing as readily as hitting balls rapidly, one after another, without concentrating on what you are trying to accomplish.

When I'm working on my game, I place the practice balls behind me. This forces me to rest between shots as I bring the ball into position. I try to be methodical in my movements on the practice tee. I always aim my shots at a target, just as if I were on the course.

It's difficult to say how much a person should practice. It depends largely on how well and how much the individual is playing at the time, and on his goals in golf.

Generally speaking, I feel that anyone who plays almost every day as I do, and is playing well, should stay away from the practice tee. But if a golfer plays only once or twice a week, he should practice, even if he is playing well. The practice will help groove his swing.

The golfer who is putting well should not practice this phase of the game. When putting, it's too easy to experiment with something that might ruin a successful technique.

Above all, never practice when you are tired. You will force your swing, destroy timing and, in general, do more harm than good.

Not all practicing need take place on the practice tee or green. For instance, practicing in deep rough is a good way to develop clubhead speed. Don't use a ball; just whip the clubhead through the grass.

You will find that if you are uncocking your wrists too soon on the downswing and losing clubhead speed, your club will stick in the grass. If you swing correctly the club will go through the grass and give you the feeling of hitting through the ball.

When I'm at my home course, I often practice by using clubs other than my driver off the tee.

On a hole that normally calls for a driver and a 7-iron, I might hit a 5-iron off the tee and then a 4-wood to the green. The choice of club for the tee shot depends on what club I wish to hit to the green.

This is a good way to make someone's home course an entirely new and different challenge. It provides on-the-course practice with clubs that may be neglected. Also, this method of play helps develop the ability to judge distance.

A golfer who is pressed for time can do his game a lot of good merely by gripping and swinging a club around his house.

When I was in school, I played rugby, cricket and other sports and wasn't able to shoot much golf unless I played hooky, as truancy is commonly called in this country.

So, when I got home from school I'd swing a club on a rubber mat for a few minutes while my bath water was running. Sometimes I'd swing before leaving for school. These few minutes of practice helped me maintain my feel and timing so I could play well on weekends.

The question often arises whether a person should take lessons in addition to his practicing. My answer is always a definite yes.

Many times practicing will iron out the rough spots in a swing, but often the player will merely aggravate the cause of his golf problem by unknowingly repeating it shot after shot on the practice tee.

My advice to anyone taking a lesson is to ask the pro to first check grip, stance and weight transference during the swing. These are the foundations for good golf.

Then tell your pro how much time you can devote to your game so he will know whether to work drastic changes with your swing, or merely to remedy the current ailments. Listen carefully to the pro's advice and question him on the spot if you don't understand a part of the instruction. A good pro realizes that all pupils do not always understand his instruction.

For instance, a pupil may be uncocking his wrists too

soon on the downswing. As a cure the pro might suggest he turn his left hip out of the way.

But then the pupil might also turn his right shoulder over the ball. So, the pro would try a new approach. He might suggest the pupil pull the club into the ball with his left hand.

This might cause the pupil to move his hands too far ahead of the clubhead and hit a slice with an open clubface.

Sometimes it's a long process to arrive at complete understanding between the pupil and the pro. Once this point is reached, the pro's job is finished. Then it is the pupil's duty to practice what he or she has learned.

When I gave lessons back home, many times pupils would tell me that the last lesson had not helped them.

"How many practice shots did you hit since the lesson?" I'd ask.

Invariably they admitted they had headed straight for the course instead of the practice tee. The player who expects a lesson to "take" without subsequent practice just isn't being honest with himself or fair to his pro.

Practice can be fun. I often make a game of my practice sessions, and I suggest the reader do the same.

Say I'm practicing an intentional hook: I will hit this shot until I can hit 10 hooks in succession. If I break the chain, I must start over.

If I'm practicing low shots, I'll try to hit 10 shots under some tree limbs. If I hit the tree, I start again.

Sometimes when I'm trying to make shots land on a certain spot I imagine there is water in front of that spot.

To conclude, let me say that during every practice session you should have a specific goal, whether it be straighter shots, more distance or merely to stretch muscles before a round. Undirected practice is worse than no practice. Too often you become careless and sloppy in your swing. You'd be better off staying home and beating the rugs.

PRACTICE CHECKPOINTS

✔ Do not practice in rain and wind, unless it is absolutely necessary.

✔ Start your practice session by hitting short shots.

✔ Always practice your short game after hitting full shots prior to a round.

✔ Be methodical about your practice. Don't rush your shots.

✔ Always hit balls to some target.

✔ If you have a chronic problem, see your pro to discover what to practice. Then practice what he preaches.

✔ Every practice session should have a specific goal. Don't practice merely to satisfy your conscience.

CHAPTER 9

GEAR FOR GOLF

I THINK a golfer should buy his clubs from a golf professional. You wouldn't go to a drug store to purchase a pair of eye glasses.

The golf club is a precision instrument. Even though it has no moving parts, it is designed to fit a precision movement—the golf swing. The golf professional is trained to fit clubs for your swing, just as the optometrist is trained to fit eye glasses for your vision.

If you doubt that clubs are precision instruments, consider this fact: a piece of tape, applied to the heel of a wood club, could change that club from a swingweight of, say, D-3 to D-4. Such a slight alteration could have considerable effect on a skilled golfer's shotmaking ability.

Choosing clubs with the correct swingweight is the most important consideration in buying clubs.

Swingweight is the relationship of weight of a club's component parts—grip, shaft and head—as determined by a swingweight scale. Most pro shops have such a scale. It would be worth a minute to determine if you are using more or less swingweight than is advisable for your physique and swing.

You might even discover your clubs do not match—that they are of varying swingweights. If so, you no doubt are compensating your swing to accommodate the difference.

Major swingweight classifications are A, B, C, D and E. Each is further subdivided into 0 through 9. Generally, a D-1 driver is slightly heavier than a C-9, and D-2 is a step above D-1.

Most men golfers and some stronger women find clubs in the D-0 to D-6 class suitable. Most women use clubs in the C swingweights. A and B swingweights are primarily for youngsters and very slight women.

George Bayer (6 feet 5 inches, 240-lbs.) is the only man I know of on the pro tour who uses an E swingweight

It doesn't always follow that a large man can handle a heavy swingweight. Strength is often deceiving. Arnold Palmer, one of the strongest golfers I've ever known, changes drivers frequently but usually swings about a D-9. Yet Paul Harney, who is very slight (5 feet 11 inches, 142-lbs.), is only two steps below Palmer at D-7.

I personally feel it's wiser to use a lighter club, sacrificing some weight in order to generate more clubhead speed. I use D-6 woods and D-3 irons.

I've been told baseball players hit more home runs today, partly because they now use lighter bats and can swing faster. The same principle applies in golf.

Physique is also deceiving when considering proper club length. A 6 foot 6 inch person might need the same length club as a person who is 5 feet 6 inches. One reason for this is that the taller person usually has longer arms. Thus, his arms may reach as close to the ground as a short man's. Also, a taller person could have a more upright swing. He probably addresses his shots closer to his feet and would require less club length than a player who reached for the ball.

Clubs can be purchased in many lengths. For men, 43 inches is standard driver length, while 42 inches is normal for women. If you feel you need more distance, you might experiment with a longer driver. This should widen your swing arc and might produce greater clubhead speed. (See Chapter I).

Shaft flexibility plays a big part in a golfer's feel of the clubhead. A weak person would have very little feel with an extra-stiff shaft (X-shaft), used by such strong players as Bayer and Palmer, because he would be unable to bend or flex this shaft. Also, he would lose distance because flex at impact helps speed the ball on its way.

On the other hand, an exceptionally strong man would not use an L (the whippiest) shaft. With his fast swing he would flex this shaft so much he would have extreme difficulty controlling the shot.

Here are the various types of clubshafts:

X, the extra-stiff shaft used by only the very long-hitting players.

S or #1, the stiff or firm shaft which is good for the normal power-hitter.

R or #2, the medium-stiff shaft suitable for most men.

A or #3, the medium flex shaft employed by strong women players and lighter-hitting men.

L or #4, the whippiest shaft of all, used by most women players and older men.

I prefer extra-stiff shafts in my short irons and stiff shafts in my long irons and woods.

Your skill as a golfer is also determined largely by the lie of your clubheads. The lie is determined by the angle formed by the bottom of the clubhead and the shaft.

A short person and/or someone with a flat swing plane can use a flat lie on his clubs because he plays the ball farther away from his feet than a golfer with an upright swing. Thus he needs a flatter lie to keep the club's toe from sticking into the air. THE OPPOSITE IS TRUE FOR A TALL PERSON WITH AN UPRIGHT SWING who plays the ball near his feet.

If your club appears to have an elevated toe at the address position (lie too upright), you are flirting with hooked. If the club's heel is off the ground (too flat a lie), you are apt to slice.

Golfers plagued with slices, hooks or an inability to raise the ball into flight might ask their pro about purchasing clubs with a hook, slice or more-lofted head to combat their particular problem. They may require a special order, but they shouldn't cost any more than the standard set.

The type of grip to use on golf clubs is largely a matter of personal preference. I like the composition rubber grips I now use. They give me a soft, but firm, feel of the club. Also, I can wash them after a round so they will be fresh the next day.

Standard-sized grips are suitable for most golfers. However, the player with exceptionally long or short fingers might try larger or smaller grips than normal. A good clubmaker can alter grip size without changing the club swingweight.

Golf balls are also designed to suit players of varying

ability. And it is not always the best (most expensive) ball that is best in performance.

A beginning golfer would be very foolish if he or she paid top price for a high compression golf ball. The distance a ball travels is determined largely by the amount it is compressed by the clubhead at impact.

A tightly wound, high compression ball rebounds farther from the clubface than a low compression ball, if both are "flattened" the same amount on the clubface. However, it takes greater clubhead speed and squarer contact to compress the tightly wound ball.

Therefore, a player who hits the ball hard and squarely most of the time can use a higher-priced, higher-compression (tightly wound) ball and obtain maximum distance.

But a golfer who swings with less clubhead speed and seldom hits the ball perfectly square would be better off using a less expensive ball. These balls are not wound as tight, and thus can be compressed with less clubhead speed and a slightly off-center hit.

Also, since cold weather makes it more difficult to compress a ball, it is wise to use less compression in lower temperatures. Ask your pro to prescribe the ball which is best for your swing.

Touring professionals, who need maximum distance on every shot, usually change to a new ball on every third hole. They do this because balls lose compression quite rapidly. I can average at least 10 yards more with a new ball than I can with one I had played for 18 holes.

In addition to having proper clubs and balls, I feel that to play his best a golfer must feel well-dressed.

When I first started playing golf overseas, my trousers were all too long for me. I was very self-conscious about my appearance, especially after a Johannesburg sports writer continually mentioned how my trouser legs dragged on the ground.

At the time I had a good excuse for my sloppy appearance. I didn't have enough money to see a tailor, and I only had two or three pairs of trousers. However, after I had won some money I visited a tailor. Thereafter, I was able to devote more attention to my game and worry less about my appearance.

Some golfers feel that if they shoot a good round in a certain shirt, they have to wear that same shirt the next day. I don't believe in that bunkum at all. If a golfer gets superstitious, he'll go only one way—down. Some players may wear the same shirt for four straight days. No wonder they don't attract much of a gallery.

People sometimes ask me why it is that pro golfers hit the ball so much farther, with apparently less effort, than the average amateur.

I don't think there is one big thing the pro does which gives him this distance advantage. His extra yardage stems from many little things, such as better grip and weight transfer, longer swing arc, later uncocking of wrists, and better balance, as well as more practice and greater development and use of the golf muscles. These are all things the amateur must develop before he can compete successfully with the pros.

However, most golfers can be in the same class with Arnold Palmer and Sam Snead when it comes to equipment. All the amateur has to do is consult the nearest golf pro.

And believe me, proper equipment can make a big difference in your game.

EQUIPMENT CHECKPOINTS

✔ Always buy your clubs from a qualified golf professional.

✔ Physique can be misleading in selecting clubs of proper swingweight and shaft flex.

✔ Heavy clubs reduce clubhead speed and might decrease, rather than increase, distance.

✔ Top quality, high compression balls are often too tightly wound for the average player to compress. Ask your pro which ball is best for your game.

✔ In cold weather balls with less compression are better than those which are tightly wound.

✔ For good golf, you should feel well-dressed.

CHAPTER 10

THE WONDERFUL
WOMEN GOLFERS

WOMEN GOLFERS are wonderful.

The men may not agree with me on this score, but when it comes to women golfers I know whereof I speak. I married one.

My wife, Vivienne, was a two handicap player before we started having babies. She has played very little golf in the past few years, but I dare say she could break 80 any time she decided to give it a go.

I feel women golfers deserve to play on a course just as much as any man does. I, for one, wouldn't want to belong to a club that didn't allow women. They make the club a happy club.

If it wasn't for the women, we wouldn't have many parties at most of our clubs. They also support the pro shop, though some husbands may feel this is a dubious distinction.

I know that Viv was directly responsible for one of my biggest paychecks in golf.

It was at the 1958 U.S. Open in Tulsa. I had a 75 the first round—putting very badly. After the round, Viv, who had followed me all the way, pointed out that I was lifting my putter on my backswing. Thanks to this sound advice I finished second in the tournament behind Tommy Bolt.

Many women try hard to appear disinterested in winning at golf. They are afraid they will appear too competitive, too masculine.

They should forget it. Few things delight men more than to see a woman who is serious about her game stand on the tee and bang away at a drive with everything she's got. The psychological reason for this is really quite simple.

Men regard golf as being almost sacred. It's a challenge to be encountered seriously, with no folderol. It offends most men to see women profane their holy cow by turning golf into a mere continuation of bridge table irrelevance.

I don't mean women should make it a habit to play a golf course with a stone face, looking like a Ben Hogan. However, I do feel that to gain acceptance from the male guardians of golf's Grail, women had better start playing to win.

On the tee, the woman golfer should forget she is chairman of the junior auxiliary. She should address that ball with knees bent and hips ready to swivel. The woman who daintily stands up to the ball, with back and legs stiff like a crusty old school marm, is just asking for a rough time from the men in the next foursome.

Very often the woman who usually is a stickler for details suddenly becomes very careless on the green. She avoids squatting to look at a putt's line. She seems to feel that the girls might think she actually cares and wants to win.

Women seem to have a physical advantage over men when it comes to the short game. They have a much more sensitive touch—if properly developed—around the green. It's a shame that so often they waste this talent by trying to be ladylike.

Now, if I have convinced any woman that she should be serious about golf (and I hope I haven't enraged too many who already are), let's see what we can do about lowering scores.

First, women should not use men's clubs. A woman's big problem in golf is lack of distance. Stiff-shafted men's clubs only minimize the yardage a woman will achieve off the tee.

Most women, unless they are in the championship class, should use whippy-shafted clubs. They need the additional clubhead speed such shafts provide.

The need for distance also dictates that women should employ a strong grip.

Right-handed women should see two or three knuckles of their left hand when they grip the club; not one or two as is standard for men. Also the V formed by the thumb and forefinger of the right hand should point to the right shoulder, rather than to the chin as with men. Thus, the woman's grip has both hands turned farther to the right on the club than does the man's.

This makes it easier for the woman to hit a ball that curves slightly from right to left in a draw or slight hook. Such a flight pattern provides more roll and distance than does a straight shot or slice. (Reverse for the left-hander, of course.) *Women should never slice.* A slice, especially in the wind, eats up too much yardage.

If a woman is just starting golf, I would advise considering the 10-fingered grip. This grip has all fingers on the shaft, instead of one overlapping as in the standard Vardon grip. More fingers on the club will allow the woman to take a fuller swing while still holding firmly onto the club.

However, when using the 10-fingered grip it is important that both hands are close together on the shaft, so they can work together as a unit. Make sure the left thumb fits snugly into the right palm.

It is true that women lack distance on golf shots largely because they are not as strong as men. However, they do have distance-producing advantages over men golfers that should be incorporated into their swings.

These advantages are suppleness, especially in the torso, and rhythm. They allow the woman golfer to take a smooth and full backswing with maximum turning of the hips.

So many women address the ball with the back and legs straight. A slight bending from the waist and knees will encourage a full body turn and weight transfer without sway.

The sway is the bugaboo of many women, as well as men. In swaying, the hips and shoulders move laterally to the right on the backswing, instead of turning or swiveling.

Most women while sweeping with a broom can feel their hips turning as they take the broom back and through. This is the same turning feeling they should have with their hips in the golf swing.

A full tilting and turning of the hips and shoulders—without sway—will coil the big muscles of the torso and legs. These muscles when uncoiled on the downswing are the ones that give maximum power in the golf swing.

Strong men golfers can hit a long ball with little hip turn, relying primarily on their better-developed arm and shoulder muscles. However, a woman golfer should strive for a full coiling of her body and leg muscles on the backswing to supply maximum power and clubhead speed.

A full turn sort of "cocks the bow." Then a quick shifting of weight to the left side at the start of the downswing releases the bowstring into the ball. This shifting of weight to the left side is very important. If the weight remains on the right side, even a perfect coiling on the backswing is wasted.

Women golfers are often accused of overswinging—taking the club back too far on the backswing. I feel that no golfer overswings unless she loosens her grip on the club with her left hand. I tell women golfers to swing the club back as far as possible—without swaying to the right and without releasing grip pressure.

Many women golfers also have a tendency to break their wrists too early on their backswing. This also destroys power in the swing because an early wrist break on the backswing usually causes an early uncocking on the downswing.

The backswing should start with the club, hands, arms, shoulders, body and legs going back as a unit. Swing the clubhead back low to the ground as far as possible without swaying the body. This will give the swing a nice wide arc.

If one takes the club back as a unit, there should be no worry about wrists breaking at the proper time. This will occur naturally as the tilting and turning of the body and shoulders raises the club off the ground.

Women who are really serious about their golf will be amazed at the extra distance they can derive from a few simple exercises. Squeezing tennis balls a few minutes a day and doing a few pushups will work wonders.

They will strengthen the grip so that one can take a longer backswing without releasing pressure on the club. They will improve hand and wrist action on the downswing so that the ball moves from right to left instead of slicing to the right.

The housewife's ironing board can aid in this exercising. Place the seat of a chair under each end of an unopened ironing board. Then lay on your back on the board, grasping a brick or similar object in each hand. Lower your hands to the side below the board and then, with arms extended, raise the bricks over your head. A great exercise for the bust line!

These exercises will not produce huge masculine muscles. However, they will improve muscle tone. They will not only help in golf but also will improve one's appearance by removing flabby flesh.

Women golfers are often the victims of too much advice —especially from male players. Unless your husband is a low-handicap player, I would take his advice with a grain of salt. Your pro is the person to see if you want first-hand golf instruction.

Well-meaning husbands should go along with this advice and encourage their wives to spend more time at golf. As a husband, I know what golf can do to improve domestic relations in the household.

Golf teaches women many qualities that might be slighted in their everyday duties as a housewife. On the course a woman learns how to compete and to accept victory and defeat. She learns how to be patient and to control her emotions. She learns quickly that you can't fly off the handle and expect to play good golf.

These are lessons that will make a woman a better mate

and mother. She will suddenly become sympathetic to a husband's golf problems. She might even understand when he leaves the lawn uncut to play a round with the boys.

Who knows, men, she might even help you win a tournament by pointing out some putting fault. Stranger things have happened.

WOMEN GOLFERS' CHECKPOINTS

✔ Clubs with whippy shafts will increase distance for most women.

✔ Women golfers should use a "strong" grip with both hands turned to the right on the club.

✔ Women should hit the ball with a slight right-to-left flight pattern.

✔ Beginning women golfers should consider the 10-fingered grip.

✔ Address the ball with a slight bending at the knees and from the waist.

✔ Make a full turn on the backswing with no body sway or lessening of grip pressure.

✔ Swing the club back with a unified, one-piece motion. Avoid early cocking of the wrists.

✔ Exercises will add distance and improve your appearance.

✔ Don't take too much advice from non-professionals.

CHAPTER 11

GOLF AND GOLFERS
AROUND THE WORLD

IN MY comparatively short golf career I've made seven world tours. I must be quite close to the million-mile mark in air travel alone, if I haven't passed it already.

Thus, I guess it's inevitable that people ask: who is the world's best golfer? What is the world's best course?

I find it difficult to pick the best golfer. Choosing the world's finest course requires less hesitation.

First let me say that in naming a "best golfer" I can consider only those who still compete. There are too many varying factors to compare Vardon, Hagen and Jones with Palmer, Snead and Hogan. If someone says that Mr. Jones was the greatest player who ever lived, I certainly would be the last to disagree.

Of the current players I rank Arnold Palmer No. 1 and Sam Snead No. 2.

Like most American players, Palmer appears to swing with little regard for style. He places more emphasis on result than on how he looks achieving it. I think of myself as the same type of player.

It is primarily Arnold's great fighting spirit that places him above Sam in my book. Also, I feel that Palmer is a bit stronger and straighter off the tee and a better putter than Sam. However, I must add quickly that Snead's tee and green games leave little to be desired. Anyone who says Sam is a bad putter should just try him sometime.

I rate Palmer and Snead at the top since both have proven their ability to play winning golf anywhere in the world.

I hear a great deal of talk about what fine golfers we have in the British Commonwealth. We do have some good ones. I won't mention any names, but I can't see many of them doing well outside of their own country. I can't think of English golfers who would be serious challengers outside of England where they know the conditions and feel confident.

I hastily add that Kel Nagle of Australia is a good player outside of his own country, as is Peter Thomson, though Peter has not shown too well in the United States. Stan Leonard of Canada is another player who has succeeded on courses all over the world. However, in my mind, I group Stan with American golfers since he has been so influenced by the American pro's style of play.

Bobby Locke, in my opinion, is the best foreign golfer to have ever competed in the United States. As you know, Locke has a very unorthodox swing. He takes the club back very much inside the target line. His club points to the right of the hole at the top of his swing. He hooks every shot.

All that doesn't worry me too much. The most important thing in golf is to have the same swing every time.

All great players have different swings. Snead's is upright; Hogan's a bit flat. Henry Cotton has a short swing—someone else's will be long. Some use an open stance; some are closed. Some, like Locke, take it back inside. Others, like Dutch Harrison, go outside. Who can say which is correct?

All that really matters in the end is whether or not you are correct at impact. And also whether you have a repeating swing.

Locke is without doubt the greatest chipper and putter I have ever seen. If he had been 30 yards longer off the tee, I'm quite sure he would have become the first golfer to score consistently in the 50's.

I'm sure Locke's steady play stems in large part from his relaxed demeanor. Everything he does is methodical. As he plods along between shots you almost hate to speak for fear you'll wake him up. If I ever saw him display anger during a round, I would be so shaken I'd blow the whole competition.

Locke was my partner in the 1960 Canada Cup matches at Portmarnock in Ireland. He was still not 100 per cent fit after his auto accident, but his play in that tournament was a study in patience.

At all times, he drove with a brassie or 3-wood. While others of us were trying to hit it a mile, all he attempted to do was keep the ball in the fairway.

We'd knock it 300 yards into that terrible heather and have to chip out. He'd hit it 220 down the middle and be in position to reach the green. Though I was outdriving Locke by as much as 80 yards, our final scores were identical.

Since we are mentioning bests, I want to say that the

best golf swing I've ever seen belongs to Ben Hogan. Except for his current bad putting, I would have placed him even ahead of Palmer in my ranking.

Hogan takes the club straight back and comes through the ball from the inside. He has excellent hip movement and always brings his right shoulder well under on the downswing. I also like the wide arc of his swing and his beautiful, long and high follow through. With this swing it is no wonder he has such great control over the ball.

Snead also has a good swing—in fact, a true picture swing. But he does not drive as straight as Hogan. I have played with Snead several times in the U.S. Open and personally feel that his sometimes erratic tee shots are the main reason why he has never won this championship.

There is no doubt that Snead is one of the greats in golf —maybe the greatest, if you look at the records. He has won more than 100 pro events. I must say, however, that I'd rather have Hogan's record than Snead's.

I think the Masters, U.S. Open, British Open and PGA are the most important tournaments. I'd rather win those once than any other 20 tournaments on the U.S. tour.

It is without hesitation that I pick the Augusta National Golf Club as the finest course I have ever played. This course has everything. If they lengthen its rough and narrow its fairways, no one would shoot better than 295 in the Masters.

The holes at Augusta offer great variety. Some fairways are fairly flat, others are undulating and some are downright hilly. The greens share this diversification.

On the 13th and 15th par-5 holes the golfer has a choice; whether to try to clear the water and reach the green in two or play short of the hazard.

On these holes, as on all great par-5s, the golfer who hits two fine shots can reach the green in two and have a chance for an eagle or an almost certain birdie.

On the other hand, the player can still achieve an easy par if he decides to play short of the water. However, the golfer who gambles and makes a bad shot can finish with a bogey or worse.

It's the same pattern on all of Augusta's holes: a good shot is rewarded; a bad one is penalized. Safe play usually will produce a par. This, along with its natural beauty, makes Augusta a great course.

I cannot say the same for the Old Course at St. Andrews, thought by many to be a great course. At St. Andrews a golfer may hook his tee shot badly and still be in position to shoot to the green. His opponent might bang one out 300 yards, straightaway, and discover his ball has finished on a sharp downhill lie or in a hidden sand trap.

And those bunkers at St. Andrews are really something. Some have sides so steep and so covered with deep grass that you actually hit backward to get out. Imagine trying to hit a ball out of your bathtub and you'll have an idea of golf at St. Andrews.

In other words, St. Andrews does not reward precision and penalize inaccuracy as consistently as a top course should—and Augusta does.

A big fault I find with many courses in America is that they appear too man-made. They lack natural terrain and show little imagination in their makeup. However, I think St. Andrews goes too far the other way. It's too natural— ancient might be a better word. Playing there gives one the feeling he is playing a course fashioned by shepherds of centuries ago—and that no one has improved it since.

But one can't help being impressed with the golfing atmosphere and tradition that abounds at St. Andrews. It truly is the home of golf, and everybody in town plays and understands the game. You can go out to the course at 10 in the evening and still find 500 people there.

I have been fortunate to play many other fine courses around the world. I hesitate to name some of the outstanding ones because I know I'll leave out many that should be included.

However, some that come to mind are Wentworth and Muirfield in Great Britain, Paruparuam G.C. in New Zealand and the Royal Johannesburg East G. C. and the Durban C. C. in South Africa.

Perhaps the one area in the world with the greatest concentration of fine courses is the sand belt area of Australia. There you have about 20 excellent courses almost on top of each other. All are in top condition, despite the fact that there are only three men assigned to maintaining each course.

As a contrast, in South Africa, where labor is cheap, a single course may have a labor force of 100.

The same is true in Japan where each player in the group has a girl caddie. Then there will be three more girls following a foursome. These girls replace divots and scatter sand and grass seed over them so that new grass will take hold.

I enjoy golfing in any country, but I must say that the best turf for golf is found in England, where there is so much moisture in the air.

There the fairways are close-cropped and the grass is so thick you get good lies, even with the small English ball. Also, the turf is firmer there. When you hit an iron shot, the entire divot remains intact. You can replace it and hardly find the spot from which it was taken by the golfer.

America has the best-groomed courses. They are really immaculate. I do feel, however, that green superintendents allow the grass to grow too long on most American fairways. (This remark does not include the great American courses such as Augusta and Pinehurst).

On most American fairways the ball nestles into the grass, making shots difficult to control. A shot sometimes seems to fly forever in the United States because the long grass and spongy turf make it difficult to apply proper backspin.

The lush fairway, to my thinking, is not so wonderful as so many club members think. I like a fairway where the ball sits up and where you feel solid contact with your club when it cuts into the turf.

Americans tell me they do not cut the fairways short or for fear they will burn out. I disagree. I think that during the growing season the fairways should be close-cropped so that dew, rain and sprinkler water can seep down to the roots and nourish the whole plant. When the fairways are long, the moisture rests on the top of the grass until the sun dries it out.

I will say, however, that I prefer American greens to those in England. They don't believe in watered greens over there. It is rare when you can fly a long shot all the way to a green in England. About the only time it is possible is during or immediately after a rain. It is easy to see why British players excel at the pitch-and-run game, while Americans prefer pitching all the way to the hole.

There is one advantage to British greens. Because they are hard and because the grass is so thick, they seldom show spike marks. This is not true of the watered American greens.

Still, I'll take the watered greens and fairways. Just cut them a bit shorter, please.

If there are variations in courses around the world, there are also differences in style of play.

I'm not amazed that many American golfers become discouraged when they find it takes them five or six hours to play a round of golf.

Crowded courses are partly the reason. However, I find American amateur golfers extremely slow even when the course is comparatively clear. A five-hour four-ball match is almost unheard of elsewhere in the world. I'd say that 3½ hours is about average for 18 holes.

I don't criticize a player for taking time to plan his shots. But there really is no excuse for the way some people dawdle down the fairway.

Swing styles also vary around the globe, although the trend in the past few years has been toward the American style. Basically, American and British golfers differ in the amount of body they employ in the swing. British golfers are largely hand players. They start the backswing largely with their hands. Americans turn their legs and body sharing the movement with the arms in a one-piece motion.

When one considers that no man has arms as strong as his legs, back and shoulders, it is easy to see a major reason why American golfers have been the more successful.

One problem for the foreign player is changing back and forth from the bigger ball played in America, to the smaller balls used in the Commonwealth. Both balls have advantages.

Generally speaking, the smaller ball is easiest to play in

a wind. For this reason alone, I don't think British golfers would care to switch to the larger ball. With the wind blowing the way it does over there, the bigger ball would really pose problems.

I can hit the British-type ball 25 yards farther into a strong wind than I can the larger ball. A cross-wind will have much greater effect on the U.S. ball. Only when driving with the wind does the larger ball have an advantage.

From the fairway the bigger ball is easier to hit. Americans would really have problems trying to dig the smaller ball out of their lush fairways.

I think the bigger ball is much better out of sand. You can really make it talk. You can attack the flag with it, whereas it is more difficult to put stop on the smaller ball.

On chip shots I also prefer the U.S. ball because I can be very firm with it. I have to be more delicate with the smaller ball because it seems to jump off the clubface much faster.

I have no preference of balls when putting. It's just as easy for me to miss them with either.

I think it would be a wonderful thing if someday the Royal and Ancient and the United States Golf Association would compromise on an in-between ball that would be standard all over the world. I know this would delight many golfers. It also would discourage the current practice of using illegal (smaller) balls in the United States.

The balls have been standardized in other sports such as baseball and tennis. Why not in golf?

CHAPTER 12

CONDITIONING YOURSELF

GOLFERS ON the pro circuit have many different ways of letting off steam from the day-in, day-out tournament routine.

Billy Casper and Julius Boros are great ones for suddenly deciding to take a day off before a tournament in order to test a nearby trout stream. Arnold Palmer is a real bug on flying and gets many invitations to go aloft with local aviators.

Movies, card games—usually bridge—and, of course, television are favorite forms of escape for other players.

I like to spend my off-the-course time with my family, listening to music and watching TV in the motel room or, as is often the case, with friends who have invited us to spend the week at their home.

But above all I like to sleep—nine hours each night, at least. Proper rest, diet, and exercise are very, very important to me.

I would like, therefore, to present my personal conditioning habits in hopes that readers will be inspired to follow suit.

Unlike most touring professionals I travel not only across America several times a year, but also to many foreign countries. The time change on a flight from one tournament to another may be three or more hours and this really affects sleeping habits.

I'm fortunate in that being young, this travel doesn't bother me too much. Also I'm blessed with the ability to sleep anywhere, especially on a plane. A friend who flew with me recently from Africa to America said traveling with me is like traveling on your own. I slept practically all the way.

When I sleep I'm really out cold. It doesn't matter what kind of a round I played that day or where I stand in the tournament. I was four strokes behind Palmer going into the last round of the 1962 Masters and I slept nine hours that night. As you know we tied the next day with Dow Finsterwald and again I slept nine hours before the play-off. The year before at Augusta I led by four strokes going into the last round. Then it rained the next day. That meant an extra night to mentally dwell on the tournament, and worry like that can be rough on the nerves. But still I slept a sound 10 hours that night.

The time I retire is determined somewhat by the time I'm scheduled to tee off the next day. But I rarely turn in after 11:30. That's very late for me unless I've had some sleep during the day. If I finish my golf in the early or mid-afternoon, I often nap for an hour or so before dinner.

The amount I sleep varies a bit and depends on climate. If I'm in Texas, where the hot sun really takes it out of you on the course, I will sleep more than if it is cooler and I hadn't burned up so much energy.

Though sleep is important to the touring professional,

proper diet is just as necessary. It is even more vital to the average golfer who spends much of his time on the job, and doesn't burn off the calories as we professionals do.

I take great pride in being trim. I like to see a woman who looks good in a bathing suit and I'm sure women feel the same way about men. I have made a personal vow that in 25 years my weight will be within five pounds of the 160 pounds it is today.

Because tee times vary on the tour, it is very easy to develop an ulcer on the golf course. A player who is scheduled to tee off at 11:30 in the morning, may have eaten breakfast at 8. He probably won't finish before 3:30 or 4 in the afternoon, so he will have gone at least 7½ hours without food.

Your body is like a motor car engine. You have to put fuel in or it runs out of gas. Therefore, I always carry some raisins in my bag and eat them during the round. They are full of energy and easy to digest.

Ideally, I try to eat about an hour to an hour and a half before I start my round. It's bad for your game to eat a big meal and then immediately start play. All the blood goes to your stomach and you feel sluggish. I have to be careful about what I eat when I'm playing in the U.S. or British Open, where you have to play 36 holes in one day. Then you have to eat enough to maintain your strength, but not so much that you get listless.

I don't follow any special diet, but I have had the opportunity to talk to many doctors on the subject. I'm convinced that fried foods and pastries are very bad. I eat a lot of fruit and vegetables and lean meat, and I drink plenty of milk.

For my evening meal I always have a steak and a baked

potato with some salad. My one weakness is hot bread. That really tastes good to me with dinner. Instead of dessert I often take some milk and chocolate ice cream back to the room and enjoy this treat just before I go to bed.

You may not believe that a touring professional would have to rely on exercises to keep fit for golf. Yet, I have found that certain exercises can help my game, no matter how much I play. I speak specifically of exercises that develop strength in the legs, back, arms and hands.

Keeping the legs in shape is very important to a golfer. I'm convinced they are the first to go as a player gets older. As young as I am, there have been times in the past when my legs have felt weak during the latter stages of a round.

Therefore, I've adopted a program of deep knee bends which I try to carry out daily. Every evening, and in the morning if I have a late tee time, I do at least 30 squats on each leg. I stand on one leg and bend down at the knee and straighten up. This has done wonders for my legs and I no longer feel tired during a round.

To develop the arms and hands it will help to work out with some sort of squeezing device. There are plenty of them on the market. I have a piece of wood with a piece of string attached and with a weight on the end. By turning the wood in my hands, thus rolling up the string and the weight, I develop the arm and hand muscles which I use in the golf swing.

I don't think it is too good to perform exercises that develop shoulder and chest muscles. In the past I have done a lot of fingertip pushups—as many as 80 at one time—but I stopped these when I found that my chest and shoulder muscles were starting to tighten and restrict a free swing of the golf club.

So you see, just as Casper and Boros escape from golf through fishing, and Palmer by flying, I keep in balance largely through a program of sleep, diet and exercise.

I'm sure my friends on the tour get relief mentally through other outside interests. However, I prefer my way because I get not only mental satisfaction but also physical well-being.

Often I have returned to my room after a tiring and discouraging day on the course. But if I do my exercises and read a good book before retiring, I really feel clean and eager to do a better job the next day.

CHAPTER 13

JUST TALKING

JUST AS American boys are weaned on baseball and football, I grew up on cricket and rugby. When I was 15, I thought golf was too tame—even a bit dull.

But my father was a two-handicap player and had long waited for the day when I'd join him for a round. One day, with nothing better to do, I decided to give it a go.

The first three holes were really very easy—a par-three and two short par-fours. I parred all three, and I don't think anything since in golf has given me a bigger thrill.

The rest of the round saw my beginner's luck run dry as I shot eights and tens and that sort of thing. But golf was in my blood.

I never was too keen about schoolwork; often I'd forsake the classroom for the golf course. It didn't take me long to decide I wanted to be a golf professional.

In this final chapter I would like to toss out some random thoughts about golf and my life as a pro.

First, a note about the most fundamental thing in golf:

I think the odds are against anyone becoming a par golfer until he employs a correct grip on the club.

When I first started, I had a very bad hooker's grip. That is, I could see all four knuckles of my left hand, and my right was way under the shaft. Most people grab a club this way the first time, just as they would grab a stick.

At first I hooked the ball all the time. Finally, I reached the point where I'd do anything to slice.

Then I went to the opposite extreme. With my new slicer's grip I could see no knuckles of my left hand, and my right hand was almost on top of the club. I cured my hook, to be sure, but I also developed a very flat swing plane as a result.

Finally I arrived at what I consider to be the perfect grip.

This finds two knuckles of my left hand visible as I look down at my grip. My left thumb lays on top of the shaft. The V formed by my left thumb and forefinger points toward my chin.

I grip largely in the fingers of my right hand so that its V points toward my right cheek. The thumb of this hand touches the end of my forefinger just to the left side of the shaft.

Thus, my palms are almost facing each other. This is the grip I would naturally assume if I were to stand with my hands at my side, palms inward, and then reach forward to grasp the club, still with the palms facing. Naturally, my right shoulder would lower a bit since my right hand grips lower on the shaft than does my left.

I recommend this grip to any man of normal strength who is under 35 years of age. For women, older men, and men of slight build, I recommend a grip that would encourage more of a hook. Such a grip would have almost three knuckles of the left hand showing. The V formed by the right hand should point to the right shoulder.

Many people shy away from any grip change because it feels unnatural and because the results are not always an immediate improvement.

All I can say is that you must have a good grip to play good golf. And nothing comes easily—especially in golf. Be patient and practice your new grip. In time it will feel natural and you will be glad you made the effort.

Most people have some criticism of their chosen profession, and golf pros are no exception. I really should be the last person in the world to complain about golf. However, I do feel the game could be improved in certain ways. I shall try to be constructive.

I feel we are losing something in golf through the growing tendency in America to place markers showing distance from the tee or to the green on the edge of the fairways. This practice all but eliminates the need to judge distance, and I feel judging distance is as much a traditional part of golf as is playing them as they lie and reading greens. I think the person who excels in judging distance should be rewarded as much as the person who correctly judges the line of his putt.

Another thing in golf that minimizes a player's ability is the rule which allows a golfer to seek and receive advice from his caddie.

Most caddies are assigned by luck of the draw. I don't think it is right that one player should benefit from the knowledge of a good caddie, while his opponent is stranded with a boy who has never before walked around a course. I say let the player rise or fall on his own ability and let the caddies merely carry the bag and keep the clubs and balls clean.

Probably I shouldn't complain about receiving advice from caddies. My Masters victory stemmed largely from the fact I had the best caddie I've ever known.

Some people may wonder how much caddies earn in a pro tournament. Few, if any, players give their caddies less than $5 per round and $1 per hour for shagging practice balls.

I don't believe I've ever paid a boy less than $90 for the six days at a tournament. My biggest payoff was after winning the Masters when I gave my boy $1,400 and some clothes and clubs. He was worth every cent of it.

In tournament golf a player is penalized for "undue" delay. I personally feel there should also be a penalty for fast players who are in such a hurry that they leave the putting green before their opponents or playing partners have holed out.

A big problem at tournaments where large galleries follow the play occurs when the gallery rushes from a position near a green to the next tee before the players have completed putting. The player who prematurely leaves the green himself only encourages such conduct by the gallery.

I walk fast between shots, but I take a good bit of time in planning the shot. If I'm playing with a fast player who rushes ahead down the fairway, I find I must fight against rushing my own tempo of play.

In fact, one of the reasons I strive for long drives is to assure outdriving others in my group. That way I can think about my second shot while those who had shorter drives are executing their seconds. In this way I don't feel I'm delaying the play of anyone who wants to race around the course.

Another thing I'd like to see changed in golf would be to have the rules for the Ryder Cup matches between American and British pros revised so that all Commonwealth golfers could play on the British side.

I know the British pros will not go along with this thinking; largely, I'm afraid, because many realize they would have difficulty finding a spot on a Commonwealth team.

But let's face it: the Americans have pulverized the British in the Ryder Cup. It's getting to be a question, not of who will win, but by how much.

Such competition is bound to die on the vine sooner or later. Today the matches fail to command the prestige they once did.

And I don't think that limiting Ryder Cup matches to 18 holes will help create interest. The Ryder Cup should determine the best players, and the best player is more likely to win over 36 holes than over 18.

Unlike some people, I try not to criticize a golfer who has attention-getting mannerisms. I think golf needs colorful players.

In a way, Tommy Bolt has done a lot of good for golf. He has brought many people out to see tournaments who otherwise would not have attended.

I recall at one tournament my family and I stayed at the home of some friends. Our hosts had not planned to watch the tournament until one of their young boys said: "Mommy, take me out to see the bad man (Bolt). I want to see him play."

Tommy may lose his temper a bit, but it doesn't bother

me because he never interferes with my play. The only person he hurts is himself. He is one of the finest golfers that ever lived, and there is no telling what he would have done if it wasn't for his temperament.

I guess I shocked a few people some time back when I competed in trousers that had one leg black and one leg white. I still get a little embarrassed when I think about it.

However, those pants served a good purpose. Pictures of me playing found their way into newspapers and magazines around the world. I like to think those pictures encouraged some people to attend a golf tournament when I played in their area.

It's the same with the Elvis Presley routine I did on the Perry Como television show after winning the Masters. With millions watching in the TV audience, I felt my singing would do more to promote golf than I ever could have done by merely answering questions.

I had always heard that America is the land of opportunity. This is certainly true as far as the golf pro is concerned. It's really wonderful the way the people in the United States treat foreign players. In tournaments I never have the feeling the gallery is pulling against me because I am not an American. I also have been treated admirably by the fellows on the pro tour.

It is quite expensive to play the American tour. I figure it costs me nearly $1000 a week to travel with my family and a nurse for the children.

With the money available to a winning player in this country, it is no wonder competition is so tough. Any time I finish among the top 10 in an American tournament I feel I've done remarkably well. I can assure you that the man who finishes 10th hasn't played much worse than the

man who won. I never cease to be amazed at the amount
of time American pros spend on their games. They deserve
to be the best in the world.

My big ambition in golf is to someday win the U.S.
Open. I think I will if I stay healthy and get a few breaks.

But if I don't win the Open myself I can help my infant
son, Mark, to that goal. However, I will not force golf on
my children. I will encourage them if they show an interest, but it's entirely up to them.

Some day, when I'm finished with golf, I'd like to return
to South Africa and do some farming. I have a small farm
now in Johannesburg which my brother-in-law runs for
me. I don't think I'd want, however, to depend on farming
for a complete living, because of the worry about weather.
I'd like to make it a hobby.

Since that day 11 years ago when I first ventured onto
the course, my whole life has been wrapped up in golf.
Well, maybe that's a bit strong. I always try to put my
family first. But sometimes it isn't easy. Often, I feel like
I'm being torn apart.

One week I might be in England playing a television
match with Arnold Palmer at St. Andrews. The next week
I might be in Hollywood for a guest appearance on another
TV show. Somewhere in between I might be committed to
appearances on behalf of products I endorse.

There will be countless invitations to banquets and cock-
tail parties. I hate these occasions. Usually there is a lot
of speechmaking in smoke-filled rooms. And then there are
the autograph hounds. They never seem to stop.

Along with all this I must keep a fine edge on my golf
game. Anyone who has played the game seriously knows
that this, in itself, is a full-time job.

Finally, there is my wife, and the children. Sometimes I don't see my daughter Jenny, who is three, for several days. When I leave for the course, she often grabs my leg and cries. She is afraid I might be leaving on another trip.

When I was a teen-ager and dreamed of winning the British Open and the Masters, I thought only of the glory and the money. I never realized that some day I would have a daughter who would cry.

But there is another side to the coin.

I have made more money during my few years in golf than many men make in a lifetime.

I have traveled around the world and seen places and played courses most people visit only in their imagination.

I have made wonderful friendships—enough to last a lifetime.

And I think I've had the pleasure of making a few people happy. Occasionally I object to signing autographs, but it all becomes worthwhile when I note the joy in some youngster's face.

Someday, some child to whom I spoke words of encouragement may be challenging me for the U.S. Open title. I sincerely hope so.

I owe a lot to golf. It's a debt I'll never be able to repay.

CHAPTER 14

A LAST WORD

THE ability to adapt himself to changing circumstances is one of the most important skills any golfer can have. I have realized this fact for a number of years, but it was never brought home to me so graphically as in the 1962 Professional Golfers' Association championship on the Aronimink course in Newton Square, Pennsylvania.

In the Western Open a few weeks before the PGA tournament, I had experimented with using a 4-wood off the tee on certain holes. Previously, on the pro tour, I had very seldom replaced a driver with a 4-wood, believing that the fifteen yards difference in distance was too much to give up. But Aronimink is one of those courses where there is a tremendous premium on accuracy. The rough is thick and there are numerous trees and traps lining the fairways. And anyone knows that a straight ball is the hardest shot to hit in golf.

I figured that I could use the 4-wood to reach the green with my second shot, while the other fellows were hitting irons. If you're playing well, there's no reason you can't do this.

I don't mean to say that I'm not always striving for length. But many players forget that it is often more important to keep the ball in play.

Chick Harbert says that every golfer must have one bread-and-butter shot, something that he can fall back on when nothing else will work. I guess that my 4-wood falls into that category for me, although this may be only a phase. In another year it could be something entirely different. But in the PGA I used the 4-wood off the tee on 21 of the 72 holes.

I made another alteration in my game at Aronimink. A day or two before the tournament, I was watching Bill Casper practice on the putting green, paying particular attention to the way he broke his wrists. I noticed he was employing a firmer stroke than me—a jab, with a short follow through. I had previously made a move in that direction, but my putting was still not going well, so I decided to adapt my style more closely to Casper's.

Putting is extremely important to the game of golf, and this fact is realized by the top pros. I think the main difference between the tournament scores of today and 20 or 30 years ago is that the pros spend ever so much more time practicing on the greens.

Anyway, the changes I made worked, and I was fortunate enough to win the PGA with a score of 278, although Bob Goalby made me sweat by coming close to a tie on the 72nd hole. I felt very lucky that, by the age of 26, I had won the Masters, the British Open and the PGA.

I would like to close with a story about a young man back in Johannesburg. We had an African shop boy at

Gary Player and his tools. He prefers a 44-inch driver, slightly longer than average.

Golf is constantly on Player's mind. Here he checks his grip on an imaginary club before signing scorecard after a round.

Gary blasts from one of the mammoth traps of Australia's Royal Melbourne course, which he rates as one of the world's finest.

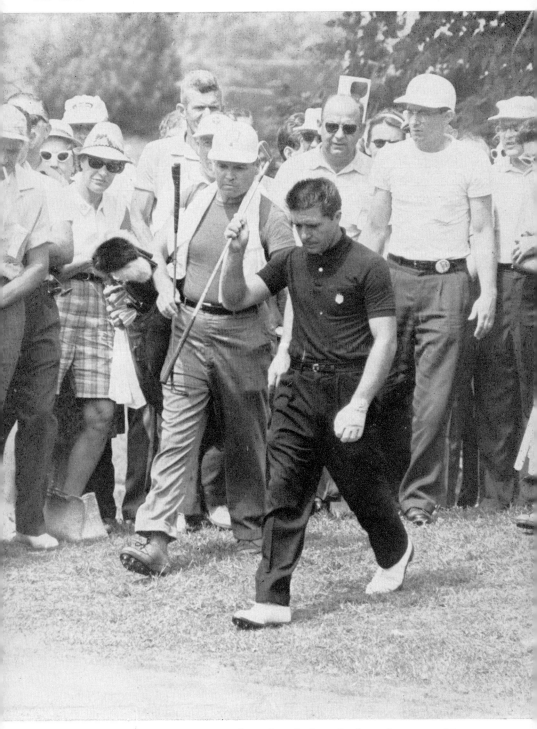

Gary sometimes paces off shot to direct his thinking back to the competition.

Though Gary is a firm believer in yogi exercises, such as standing on one's head, he finds insufficient time on the tour to develop a yogi routine day to day.

Gary feels that the grip should be a natural thing. To take it properly, merely stand with hands at sides (upper left), bring hands forward in front of you—palms still inward (upper right), then merely put hands on the club (lower left). This gives proper grip with palms practically facing each other on the club.

the Killarney Country Club named William. He couldn't
read or write when we hired him, but he was teaching himself how to read by poring over every golf book or magazine that came into the shop.

Often I found him before a mirror practicing the strokes
he had learned. He knew the records of almost every golfer
in the world, much as a youngster in America can reel
off the batting averages of all the baseball players.

Bobby Locke and I were scheduled to play a three-day,
head-to-head challenge match. He had never been beaten
in South Africa in this kind of match, and I was quite
nervous. I asked William if he thought I'd beat Locke.

"No," he said, "you can never do that. You will be too
frightened with such a great player."

"But I'm putting very well," I said. "Especially the short
putts."

"You're putting very badly. Bobby Locke will kill you
on the greens. He is a wiz-ard with that putter. You are
too young and you will be too scared."

The morning of the match I called the shop to see if
anyone wanted a lesson. When William answered the
phone, I thought I'd pull his leg. He said, "This is William,
the shop boy."

I disguised my voice and introduced myself as Bobby
Locke.

"Good morning, Mr. Locke."

"How's Gary Player playing these days?"

"Oh, very, very well," said William.

"How is he putting?"

"He's putting like a wiz-ard," William said, using the
same inflection in his voice as he had with me.

"Thank you very much," I said, changing my voice,

"this is Gary Player." There was a momentary silence on the other end of the phone, and suddenly I heard a click.

When I walked into the shop later that morning, William buried his face in his hands to keep from laughing.

I shook my head. "William, I'm surprised at you."

His hands dropped to his side. "One things is sure, Mr. Player. Self-praise is of no recommendation."

I will leave the reader with that piece of wisdom from my native country.